Live, Love, Learn
and Leave a
Legacy—

Dr Berg

IS YOUR LIFESTYLE KILLING YOU?

YOU?

HOW TO CHASE YOUR DREAMS WITHOUT SACRIFICING YOUR HEALTH & SANITY

DR. CHARLES BERG

published by

duffin|creative

los angeles

Published in the USA by
Duffin Creative
11684 Ventura Blvd #205
Studio City, CA 91604
Visit us on the Web at duffincreative.com

ISBN-10: 0615882587
ISBN-13: 978-0615882581

Printed in the United States of America

Table of Contents

Acknowledgments

The writing of this book was more a spiritual experience than a literary one. The act of putting my thoughts on paper allowed me to place meaning on moments. Looking into the rearview mirror of my life allowed me to see the serendipitous events and how there was a divine carpet ride that had led me to this very moment.

I want to thank every person I've met in my fifty-four years. That would be quite a task to enter each of your names. However, I've learned that every human interaction does something to alter the very substance of who we are.

Dearest Mom in heaven, thank you for giving me the greatest gift a child could receive. You were the perfect "nudge." You helped me understand that I had capacities greater than what I saw in myself. You were taken from us too soon, but I can see your smile and forever feel your love.

Dad, you never realized the gift of your own writing and creativity. I dedicate this book, as a tribute to you, for showing me how to be a compassionate and loving being. You were the epitome of non-judgment. Your quiet, yet deep unspoken love was felt every moment of my life. I've learned that words can be cheap. Although you were quiet, your love was ever present and supported me through all of life's tribulations.

Ruth, we spent the better part of thirty-five years together. I learned so much from our relationship. Thank you for the greatest gifts I've ever received—our children.

To my children, Jason and Lindsay. I hope that one day each of you has the opportunity to rear and nurture your own offspring. Jason, you are my hero. I talk about the philosophies of personal responsibility. However, you live them every day of your life. Thank you for the incredible gift of you, a son who has epitomized "turning obstacles into stepping-stones." Lindsay, thank you for being everything I could have wished for in a daughter. Your beautiful smile and contagious laugh heals me when life feels overwhelming. I so appreciate your reminding me, "Daddy, stop reading and start writing!" Your incredible heart and empathetic ways are felt by everyone.

Thank you, Jeff Kirsch, for being the most supportive and encouraging friend. Your concern, compassion, and unselfishness are overwhelming. You've been a pillar of strength for me and have so supported my professional and personal life. You're one quality "dude" and I love you.

To my wife Jody, you're the "wind under my wings." You're the invisible force behind this book and the world needs to know it. You believe in me more than I believe in myself. I needed someone to ignite my passion when my "pilot light" was sputtering. Thank you for your unconditional love, for making me smile every day, and most importantly, for so supporting my message and helping me discover my authentic voice. Hang on to the "magic carpet"; we're going for a ride. I don't know where it's taking us, but we're going to alter the lives of many people.

I need to thank my high school swim coach, Doug Stern. Who knew that a few words in my high school year book would have such power? "Chuck, you have leadership capabilities—believe in yourself." Your desire to help me was an incredible jump-start to my personal entrepreneurship. I'll eternally be grateful for "showing me the way."

To all my mentors at New York Chiropractic College, thank you: Dr. Ernest Napolitano, Dr. Frank DeGiacomo, Dr. Marty Greenberg, Dr. Phil Striano, Dr. Frank Nicchi, Dr. Larry Markson, Dr. Danny Drubin, Dr. Dennis Perman, and Dr. Bob Hoffman.

While attending the final class at the Institute of Integrative Nutrition, the founder of the school, Joshua Rosenthal, urged the attendees to go out and create a change in this world and to "get it done in this lifetime." Joshua, thank you for those words. You're a force for good on this planet This book is a ripple effect of your vision. I appreciate you.

To Dr. Michael Chimes for introducing me to the field of chiropractic. In twenty-four hours, my life was altered forever. Thank you for your enthusiasm and passion for this wonderful science. In our first meeting, you saw a connection between me and my potential to make an impact on other people. Chiropractic was the venue and I'll always be grateful.

Iris, you've been more than a sister to me. You're always an amazing listener who cares and supports. Thank you for teaching me non-judgment and unconditional love.

As an author and editor, Mike Lewis knew there was a story inside of me. Mike, thank you for helping me realize my ability and capacity to express a very important message to humanity. Your encouragement has come to fruition.

More than twenty years ago, I shared my thoughts and philosophies with my patient and friend, Jeff St. John. Thank you, Jeff, for acting as a reflection of faith, confidence, and belief, and for your incessant reminders to me of how valuable my messages were to your personal transformation. You reminded me that "a candle loses nothing by lighting another candle."

Finally, I want to thank the hundreds of authors whose books I read and shared their interpretations of how to survive Life 101. May you challenge yourself to sit down and put your own spin on living an empowered life. None of us has a copyright on living. Go for it! Grab a pen and paper, or a mouse and screen. You too have a gift you need to leave behind.

§

A Message about Dr. Berg

In this book, Dr. Chuck Berg takes you on a journey that enables you to clearly visualize that everything you need to change on the path you are on, you already have within you. Through his compassion for life's miracles and his ability to express his inner voice, he is truly an agent of change. In his kind, soft-spoken, but direct and loving deliverance of a way of thinking and approaching life, you feel immediately less anxious and more focused as to how to move forward. If you have a chance to attend one of Dr. Berg's seminars, you'll find the experience much like reading this book: At the end, you'll feel that you are OK just the way you are and that getting better is not as difficult as you thought it would be. In fact, Dr. Berg brings a certain level of excitement to what your future could hold.

Dr. Berg's presentation style is very personal: he exposes the challenges he was faced with, both professionally and personally, making him extremely approachable. He speaks to you as if no one else was in the room and his entire message is directed toward you. His comforting nature, warmth, and sincerity make you feel as if you have known him for a lifetime,. He has a way of making you feel good about yourself and helping you identify and own your strengths. He shows you that the challenges that are placed in your life are stepping-stones toward growth, rather than barriers in your pathway. He discusses how simplifying your life allows you to reach down and face the core of your existence, and how to lower the distracting noise of everyday life so that you can focus on developing your inner voice.

How has his message changed me?

In the past, when I have listened to other speakers or read their books, at times I have felt revved up from the message they were delivering. But soon after, I felt pressure to follow their advice. If I fell short, I was left feeling like a failure because what they were recommending, I was unable to do. They were telling me what to do, rather than sharing what they have done to become successful in their spiritual, emotional, physical, and mental worlds.

Dr. Berg is different!

He is not telling you what to do to change your life. He is merely sharing with you some of the methods he has used to achieve the serenity that he lives with on a day to day basis. He shows you how each and every one of us is no different than he is, and that we each have the capacity to achieve this inner sense of harmony by being positive and taking the steps to face each situation without fear, without judgment, and without an agenda. When you've finished reading this book you'll have an appreciation for the moments you have, an acceptance for the moments that have passed, and a sense of hope for the moments yet to come.

Most importantly, Chuck is a regular guy, sharing his regular life, which has been more complicated than some and less than others. Yet he appears comfortable in his own skin, no matter the situation that faces him.

When you see someone who appears to have such a handle on life—such confidence that no matter what was in his way he can handle it—you want to be like him. So when you hear his message, you'll want to live as he does and achieve his level of security. There is no one I have met, as of yet, that, when I tell them I am a good friend of Chuck Berg's, hasn't said, "What a truly nice guy—a wonderful person—I've always liked him." That does not happen by accident. His desire to help people by sharing with them one by one is his purpose in life—along with loving those in his immediate circle.

You feel equal to him, not as if he is the teacher and you the student. He removes the barriers between himself and his audience by speaking directly to you, and most importantly, by genuinely caring about you. His seminars—and this book—do not feel like a lecture, but rather like a learning experience in which you know when you leave the room, something was lifted off your shoulders. You are enlightened to yourself rather than to his "theory on life." You have a direction of where your next step might be, but no pressure to do it, and an excitement to want to do it because you know you can. He speaks of believing that you can do anything you set your heart to rather than your mind, and it is obvious that he has set his heart toward reaching out to those around him and helping them to make a difference. I know Chuck can, he is, and he will continue to do so. He has made his fantasies into dreams and his dreams into realities.

There is an expression that says some people enter your life for a reason, some for a season, and some for a lifetime. Well, Chuck Berg is the type of person that enters for a lifetime, and leaves an impression and a message that lasts forever.

—*Jody Chimbel, OT*

Foreword

Most of us are like a phonograph needle stuck in the groove of a vinyl record, unable to move out of the same old habits. So round and round we go, never advancing. My book takes the reader on a soul-searching mission that helps facilitate answers to long sought after questions.

In a world where people hit the pavement running, we rarely see ourselves as we are. We have delusions of what we do and what we say. In essence, we live unconscious lives. As a result, we suffer consequences in our health, relationships, work, and simply stated, in our potential.

Recognition or Conscious Awareness is the very first step in our endeavor to improve ourselves and initiate a transformation.

I do my best to be an agent of change. This book facilitates and pulls from you the answers to long sought after questions about yourself. Through some riveting questions, you will find that all your answers were inside of you all this time. They always are.

What better tool could you ask for than a compilation of refreshing philosophies and time-tested wisdom to help transform your life of madness into a life of meaningful magnificence?

So get ready to lift that needle from the groove and let your New Music play!

Why I Wrote this Book

Since I began teaching at the N.Y. Chiropractic College, I've been told that I have a gift; the gift to communicate effectively and share a wonderful message. When you hear "whispers" from inside your own heart and mind, you know that these are divine messages. We all participate in jobs. Some people make careers and others have callings.

Why have I dedicated thousands of hours to read, speak, attend seminars, and make this study more important than anything else in my life?

Wisdom is priceless. It has limited value if kept hidden in a vault. It has endless possibilities if shared.

Many people don't enjoy reading. Some find it difficult. Most people can't find the time nor choose not to make the time to fill themselves with priceless philosophies.

These philosophical tenants are time-tested concepts, which, if followed and embraced, make for an incredible platform or foundation to live your life from.

Living the material that is in this book creates a table with six legs. Sturdy, rock solid, and fortified to withstand the negativity, the doubt, and uncertainty that society fills us with everyday.

Writing a book is my legacy. It's the gift I give the world to thank the universe for allowing me to participate, to dance, to cry, to love, to be hurt, to be sad, and to rejoice in giving thanks to all that I've served and who have served me.

It will be a Beacon of Light to those who really "chew" the material and ask the all-important question: How does this relate to me?

I want my children to take this material and own it. I want everyone reading this book to extract from it something that will enhance their self-esteem, something that will assist in finding their purpose, and something that touches their hearts. This, in turn, will have a ripple effect to every other person they come into contact with.

I've learned that the universe is one cosmic space. What we do, say, and think impacts everyone and everything!

I've spent time collecting, gathering, and organizing material—for what? It's obvious. To ingest, digest, assimilate, and then to produce my version of life, twenty- four hours. Is your lifestyle killing you? What are you chasing and why?

Lastly, it's important that I do this for me. If not one book is ever sold, I can say that I challenged myself to simply *do* and complete another goal.

To not listen to our inner voices, our heartfelt feelings, is to rob ourselves of our life's work!

I know what my voice is, and this book will allow Chuck Berg to live on in perpetuity.

§

Who's Reading this Book?

The most commonly used word I hear from patients, family members, neighbors, and friends is STRESS! After 37 years of working with 7,000-plus patients, I conclude with certainty that the underlying cause of almost every human ailment is the inappropriate response to the events in their lives.

This book will be sought after by the greatest percentage of the buying public, the Baby Boomers! This unique group represents about twenty-eight percent of the entire U.S. population, but more significant is that they account for more than fifty percent of our ten trillion dollar economy.

Boomers are seeking answers. People buy books to find answers to their questions or to resolve problems. They are also the most questioning generation ever, desperately pursuing solutions on how to stay young, vibrant, and more sane.

In this endeavor to get, to have, and to accomplish more, they are finding themselves frazzled, burned out, and hopelessly looking for balance.

Introduction

Have you ever asked yourself, "How can I make my life the masterpiece it was intended to be?" What if you could be the Spielberg of your own life and produce, direct, and orchestrate a life worth living?

These questions resonate with the theme of the book you are holding in your hands.

For twenty-eight years, I've dedicated myself to researching what makes successful people tick. Success has many definitions, so allow me to define success through my eyes, my heart, and my mind.

A successful human being is someone who:

1. Recognizes that life is about "we," not about "me!"

2. Understands that we are human *beings*, not human *doings*, therefore have clarity and certainty about the "who I am."

3. Defines themselves by their actions, not their words. However, their words and their actions are always congruent.

4. Recognizes that they are a spiritual being in a materialistic world and humble themselves to something bigger than they are.

If you have questions on how to become more valuable, loved, credible, and most importantly, self-loved, please read this book.

The gift of life is simply the service you give back to the infinite source.

Conscious awareness will help you see through the "cloudy lens" of "cultural software." We're a society blinded by consumption. Repeatedly, we reach for things outside of ourselves, hoping to be made more whole and satisfied by owning more things. Two mantras I've created to describe modern man are: "What I don't have is more important than what I do have" and "More is better!"

The earlier in your life that you challenge the society that is "drugging you" with its rules, its ways, and its values, the quicker your life will become more serene, peaceful, and filled with joy.

It's fascinating that although our head is only twelve inches from our heart, it seems to take almost a lifetime for the desires of these two places to align.

§

Rules

I feel compelled to ask you to return the book to the safe resting place on the shelf you took it from, unless:

- You're willing to actively participate.

- I've learned that the deepest understanding will happen when you read a paragraph or single page and write out what it meant to you. I've created questions in each chapter with an intent to make you think. I want this book to help you resurface— to move you, to shake you, and to question your current condition. What I've learned is that the more I wrote or just thought about a paragraph or concept, the deeper and more embedded was the meaning. Thus I dare you to engage this strategy and tell me if you gain an understanding and clarity that had never been there before.

- Lastly, keep a highlighter and red pen with you. Mark up the pages and rewrite what something means to you. Engage, dig deep, and articulate to others the meaning you extract from these pages. We never know how powerful a word or concept can be to our future. It's my deepest hope that you stay on course for the rest of your life visualizing and most importantly, taking action steps to live out your incredible potential.

It's the intent of this book to help facilitate your voice, your purpose for your life. Authenticity is found deep inside of you, behind your social mask, your clothes, and your possessions.

I want to ignite your pilot light, which right now is sputtering, and feed it with metaphoric oxygen and dry wood. When this happens, you'll feel the spirit rekindle inside of you.

Chapter 1

Cultural Software

"**M**ommy, how come that elephant can't move away from that little post in the ground?" I saw on television how an elephant could pull an entire tree out of the ground.

"Johnny, that's because the elephant, when it was a baby, had a chain on its leg attached to the stake in the ground." Every time it wanted to wander, it felt resistance and eventually believed it could never move away. So no matter how big and strong it is, it believed it couldn't and wouldn't even try.

Does this story remind you about yourself? What beliefs do you own that "hold you back" from taking the actions necessary to grow your unique and incredible self?

Here's what thirty years of study has taught me about being human. We're born into this world with a mind that's like a blank chalkboard. We then are subject to our caregivers (parents, most of time). It's "others" who plant our first harvest of personality, our beliefs of what's right and wrong, good and bad.

All of this "software" is downloaded into our subconscious mind. The subconscious is that part of the brain that acts as a "servant." It accepts whatever is fed to it as fact. It responds consistently with the data that it has, trusting that this data is the best available.

As we grow older, we're fed more data and more beliefs (teachers, preachers, TV, or peers) which are oftentimes conflicting with those of our original caregivers.

The reason humans have such difficulty with their minds is that there's uncertainty, based on the conflict of a variety of complicating arguments. We hear a thousand voices, like a town square where hundreds of people are talking at the same time. The clamor of all this noise makes finding truth and certainty challenging at best. Under these difficult circumstances, most of us waiver without conviction.

What is cultural software?

Think about this. The hard drive in your computer can only produce the software it is fed. Try accessing AOL when you click on Microsoft Outlook, for instance.

Humans are very complicated computers. However, our programming is very simple. Your parents and caregivers were and are your software packages. If it's true that your fundamental personality is formed in the first six years of life, a great question to raise is: "What fundamental beliefs do I possess that are deeply embedded in my nervous system?"

I don't know when we access or better yet, challenge our beliefs. However, by the time we do, it can be very difficult to lift the metaphoric needle out of the deeply- etched groove that we live in.

Cultural software is the language I use to describe the "domestication" of people. It's the societal ways, the conformity, the correct protocol to be accepted in a world where even when we disagree, we agree to please, to placate, and to not rock the boat of consistency.

The purpose of this chapter is to confront your choices, your beliefs, and simply your software package. Are you living out, day to day, your unique gifts? Are you pursuing your goals and dreams, or are they the ones society has created for you?

For most of us, we're reared to go to school, to get a good paying job, to have children, to buy a home, to take vacations, etc., etc., etc.

Rarely are we instructed to listen to "OUR" hearts, to "OUR" whispers, of the deepest thoughts that resonate from OUR passion. Rarely do we ask ourselves if our daily habits support our goals congruently?

What if our joy can't lead to our parents' vision for what they want for us? Do we default to their wishes or pay closer attention to our heart's calling?

I can't answer any of these questions. This is your homework! The greatest value of this book is the effort you choose to put into answering these questions. The power is in getting in touch with your innate software. You see, each of us is put on this planet to do something unique and incredible.

The secret is believing this! The magic is in challenging the "cultural software package" that we're given from our well-meaning parents, our teachers, guidance counselors, preachers, and rabbis, as well as our best friends (for the moment, that is).

To listen to our "inner voice" is an amazing challenge.

Cultural software teaches us that "more is better" and what you don't have is more important than what you do have. Thus, the journey of pursuit begins. More work, busyness, to get more stuff to impress our neighbors who really don't want what they have already.

Remember that cultural refers to the standard belief of the group surrounding you. It can be as broad as a global belief or it can be as limited to the five closest people you surround yourself with. There's a powerful concept that I need to bring into your awareness. "You become that which you are around most of the time." You are what your environment is. To discover how powerful and accurate this statement is, answer these questions:

1. How often did you want what your friends have? (Toys, clothes, cars, houses, jobs, second homes, or household items.)

2. What exactly are they? Name them and ask WHY you want them!

The entire advertising industry preys upon our egos. We, as a society, have been conditioned to believe that we're not good enough. In fact, the #1 fear that each of us, cross-culturally and around the world, possess is that we're not good enough.

> "Ego becomes the driving force of our lives, with our self-importance persistently taking center stage."
> —*Author Unknown*

> "Remember, most of the things you think you need are ego trips designed to bolster your image and your perception of security. You will waste a lot of energy satisfying your ego only to find that as soon as it gets what it wants, it ignores all your efforts and promptly nails another list of demands to your forehead. The ego will always try to force you to slave for its vision. I wouldn't stand for that B.S. if I were you."
> — *Stuart Wilde*

What I want you to get from this chapter is your own authentic answers to these questions.

1. Are you at peace with who you are right now?

2. Can you find contentment with where you are in your journey right now?

3. Will you find these gifts, given the complexities and pressures of your current lifestyle?

My studies have led me to understand how huge and powerful the human ego is.

Because of the inevitable basis of the ego, **I'm not good enough**, a primal sense of fear develops that can profoundly influence the way we live our lives—the goals we strive for, the people we surround ourselves with, the thoughts we think, and the dreams we make.

An *ah-ha!* that came to me more than thirty years ago was the mantra I live by today: "The most important space is the space between your ears!" Think about it.

Everything begins in thought! Therefore, what we think and what we say (self-talk) will become the manifestation of our future. Be careful what you think!

Maybe a great question to ask each of you right now is

What are your most dominant thoughts?

Stop right now and handle this question!

Profound life change happens in a moment!

I want to bring to your consciousness the reality of your present reality!

You become what you think about. Over the next five minutes, quiet yourself and allow honest, real authenticity to come through your pen and onto paper.

Here comes the Metaphoric Mission:

I'm telling you that inherent within you lie all your answers whenever you need to know them. You do not trust you, as I don't trust myself. Therefore, we ask the advice of others, believing that they know better than we do.

These exercises will help you to come out of hiding. We're playing hide and seek with our souls as we try desperately to cover up our inadequacies, our fears, and our true selves. Our social masks are but veneers, superimposed over frightened yet incredibly awesome people who have bought into someone else's dreams and goals. Welcome to the power of cultural software!

How challenging is it to endeavor to be unique? We're raised in a world to conform. We want to be liked, so we seek to "be like!"

It's my opinion that this need to "be like" blinds most of

us to the incredible individuality we all possess. Think about this. With literally billions of people on this planet, nobody has your "thumbprint." This is the reason we have our fingers and feet imprinted and stamped at birth. There's nobody in the entire world exactly like you, yet the advertising world wants to place you in a mold.

We grow up in a society that communicates a subtle message: "If you don't dress like, wear like, drive like, or live in a certain size home, you haven't made it yet!"

§

"The number of things just outside the perimeter of my financial reach remains constant no matter how much my financial condition improves. With each increase in my income, a new perimeter forms and I experience the same relative sense of lack. I believe that I would be happy if only my earnings were increased by so much and I could then have or do these few things I can't quite afford, but when my income does increase,
I find I am still unhappy because from my new financial position
I can now see a whole new set of things I don't have. The problem will be solved when I realize that happiness is a present attitude and not a future condition."
— *Hugh Prather*

Chapter 2

Living
an Unconscious Life

"Stuck in the groove of a vinyl record and unable to advance to the next song?" Wow, can you relate to this as a metaphor of your own life? Stuck at a job, in a relationship, in a "story," it doesn't matter! Humans have an uncanny habit of staying stuck, although we have no chains, no ropes, no bars, and no cement—rather, we're stuck in the fabric of our own minds.

A great question that each of us needs to pose to ourselves is: "Whose values and beliefs am I scripting my story by?"

Most of us are running on autopilot, that is, according to the rules that were handed down by our caregivers. Who am I to tell you how to live your life or by whose rules to follow? Rather, the intent of this chapter is to have you reflect or take an honest look at the rules and beliefs you have committed to. Ask yourself: How are they serving you? Are they moving you in the direction of your "true north?"

Often we find out much later in life that we lived without authenticity. We went down the path of "the many," the charted course laid down by well-meaning parents, teachers, and society as a whole. My intention here is to have you determine for yourself whether you have established RFY goals (right for you).

In my life, as I "resurfaced," that is, reflected deeply, and I found that I was following other people's goals—society's path. You know when this is happening because upon the completion or acquisition of your goal, you still feel somewhat incomplete or lacking a passionate feeling of accomplishment.

On that note, I'd like you to reflect for a moment on yourself or other people who are always tired and fatigued. It's been my observation in life that people who are tied into a job they're passionate about are rarely fatigued. When your actions are congruent with your heart's desires, the body, mind, and spirit hardly ever fatigue.

That little "pilot light" that is in each of us needs to be fed daily. Most of our pilot lights are spitting and sputtering for one basic reason. We haven't connected with what's deep inside of us. We haven't done this because society's rules have been so persuasive that we never even knew that we could challenge our beliefs and ultimately take the time to get in touch with our real desires and dreams.

Unconscious living is what ninety-seven percent of our society does every day of their lives. I started this chapter with those same words. We're so stuck in our own grooves that we don't even recognize that each day of our lives is a carbon copy of the day before!

Why do you think the same language is used by so many people when the question is asked, "Hey, what's going on?"

They answer, "SOSDD (same old stuff, different day)!"

> "Self-reflection is the school of wisdom."
> — *Baltasar Gracian Y Morales*

Scary, but true. So the value of this chapter is again not the words, but the space between the words. What does all of this mean to you?

Think about five things you find yourself doing on autopilot.

What choices "stoke" your pilot light?

Are your choices RFY (right for you) or someone else?

How do you show up on autopilot?

If you knew you could choose any dream, what direction would you go in?

Right now, honestly, are your goals yours? If not, whose are they?

Why are you living out someone else's dreams?

With pen in hand, ask yourself this question: Is what you're doing in life "soul directed" and are your goals (the things you are shooting for) "soul directed" or "society guided?"

Since you're going to invest your time (life energy), it's worthwhile to exert the minutes of your life that will never be able to be regained toward something very special.

Another way to live a more conscious life is to always remind yourself to follow your heart and not your mind. Modern science is discovering fascinating data about the human body.

Dr. Robert Cooper, in his book *The Other 90%*, shares what science is discovering with humans and their nervous systems. "Whenever you have a direct experience, it does not go directly to the brain to be thought about. The first place it goes is to the neurological networks of the intestinal tract and heart. Without getting into the complexity of the neurological pathways, let this fact simply remind you that it's important to get out of your head and get connected to the whispers that your heart and your gut are telling you. Once again it becomes a matter of trust in 'Blind Faith.'"

As I share this last statement, I find it important to have you realize that most of what goes on in your life is non-tangible! Think about this for a moment. What happens to the food you ingest? How is it converted to Life Energy to make your cells reproduce, your liver detoxify, or your kidneys extract waste? Remember, our ignorance exceeds our understanding on so many levels. My point? Stop trying to KNOW (mind).

Maybe, just maybe, this is a reason for why individuals who have such a high IQ fail so miserably in life situations or personal interaction skills. I'd love to direct anyone who finds the subject of IQ (intelligence) and EQ (emotional) to read Martin Seligman's book, *Learned Optimism*. In this wonderful piece of literature, the author explores the "explanatory style" of both the pessimist and the optimist. It's an intriguing journey to "listen" to the language of both respondents to the same problems and questions. In other words, the same life events happen to each of us. However, our reaction or response can be 180 degrees opposed. The pessimist will often see the "bad event" as all-pervasive and permanent, while the optimist will view the misfortune as a temporary setback, not his fault, and an opportunity to try harder!

Let me conclude this section by thinking deeper about this cosmic world we live in. There's another whole universe going on that we can't touch, feel, see, or completely understand. Some call it a Cosmic ATT System. Like it or not, understand it or not, it's there, and you're an integral player in this force. Remind yourself that cell phones connect by a "field" of energy. Doctors use x-rays. There's an energy coming out of that tube and into your body that you can't see, so this isn't "psychobabble." This is a universal energy, a life force—call it what you like. Just recognize that it's an energy that can work for you or against you.

I'd be remiss to leave a chapter on Unconscious Living without talking about the psychic energy you and I give off, just being ourselves.

Picture an **imaginary** antenna or cell tower coming out of your head. It's through this tower that our emotions and energies are both delivered and received. I've always found it amazing and bewildering to interact with different people and get **vibes** about these people. Come on, admit it. Of course, you've had these experiences. You have, because you too share a common nervous system, as all human beings do.

Here's what's amazing. Science has been able to measure the energy coming off of people. Years ago, the Russians developed Kurlian photography, a measure of electromagnetic energy that hovers around all living things.

To make this practical for you, allow me to share what I've learned. These fields of energy can be of different types: both positive and negative. Our body's nervous system picks up on these in a nanosecond through what we've learned earlier via our gut, our heart, and our brain.

Think for a moment of what you experienced when someone screamed at you, demonstrating immense anger or resentment. You were affected by the words, the tonality as well as the physiology of that person.

Now for a moment, think of one of the kindest and most compassionate pieces of feedback you've received.

While we all have both **positive attractor patterns** (compassion, love, nurturing, support, kindness, and peace) and **negative attractors** (anger, resentment, hatred, shame, and greed), the frequency and the volume we resonate with will proportionately determine what is returned to you in your lifetime.

How do these patterns serve you? Have they moved you toward or away from your goals?

The expression of "winning the battle, losing the war" stems from one's intimidation, size, and brawn to overwhelm the opposition (often a parent's domination over a small child). However, what often happens in life when force is used over an opponent? All too frequently, we lose love, support, and friendship when force is the equalizer.

Please list the personality traits that you can honestly say are most commonly used in your personal and business worlds. (Compassion, aggression, support, vindictiveness, etc.)

I'm hoping to have you make an honest and authentic assessment. Ask yourself if you're congruent. That is, are the personality traits moving you more toward what you want or away from your wants?

The next exercise is to find a good friend or family member and ask them to assess you. (It takes guts to give the freedom for a buddy to let you know how you "show up to the world.")

There's a fascinating expression that states: "We don't see ourselves as others see us." Therefore, be prepared to receive opinions that may be different from your perception of yourself.

Remember, this is how we grow. We must allow ourselves to be vulnerable. Otherwise, we stay "stuck in the groove" of the vinyl record, never moving on to our next song.

Can you see how this self-exploration becomes the metaphoric mirror to help you put together the pieces of your own life's puzzle, with yourself as the one with the greatest number of pieces? (Wow!)

An unconscious life is awakened if, in fact, you learned something new about yourself from doing the exercises in this chapter.

Reality teaches us that we are incredibly unconscious! To be present and in the moment is one of the greatest life challenges we can meet.

It's only when we're conscious that we can make better decisions. It's when we are conscious that we can focus on WE, and not ME.

It's the unconscious state that allows us to be cruel, to say horrific things (that we are usually guilty about moments later), and ultimately to beat ourselves up, day in and day out.

Cumulatively, unconscious states create rifts among people, poor feelings of self, and repeated actions that limit your growth on every level.

Is it worth putting more effort into staying more aware?

Not only is it worth it, but I believe it to be one of life's most important disciplines. Can I challenge you to participate in the following agreement?

"Each day I'll commit ten minutes to affirming my willingness to remind myself to stay and remain in a state of conscious awareness. It will serve me at home, at work, and with my network of friends and family."

§

"You will make more friends in two months
by being interested in other people than
you will in two years by trying to get people
interested in you."
— *Dale Carnegie*

Chapter 3

The Producer
and the Director

Over the years, we've heard the expression that each of us are the "Spielbergs" of our own lives. After all, we create our scripts, we make the choices, and collectively choreograph the dance moves we call our lives.

The question that really needs an accurate answer is whether our choices were made from our core or from the repetitive voices we've heard over the years. The sole purpose of this chapter is to get you to reflect upon your choices. To ask authentic questions and to get authentic answers will bring you to a greater level of peace and serenity. All too often, as I stated in chapter one, society's rules have permeated our souls. It became so persuasive that it created a metaphoric film over our souls. The haze and the blur of all these "got to's" and "have to's" negated the opportunity for us to allow the seed within us to germinate. If our dreams didn't conform to those of our parents, friends, grandparents, teachers, or other "authorities," those dreams simply dried up. Yet maybe they never truly dry up. Maybe our dreams stay alive and simply hibernate until the moment that we choose to break the shackles of "you can't, you're just dreaming," or "you're too young, too old, not attractive enough, or smart enough."

> "You can live a lifetime and, at the end of it, know more about other people than you know about yourself."
> — *Beryl Markham*

For just a moment, I want you to stand in front of a blank canvas. You're holding a palate of infinite colors—with brush in hand. I dare you to create your dream life. At this moment, you're the director and producer and architect of your life. Would you choose the people you're hanging with as your friends? Simply put, you'll become like the five people you hang around the most. Would you be doing the work you're currently doing? Remember, in this exercise you can't be wrong. You can't fail. You're simply here in the moment, with the job of reaching deep inside of your soul to confront your REAL feelings. We come into this world perfectly imperfect. We're then infected with "rights" and "wrongs," "do's" and "don'ts." Like an onion, we have layers upon layers of erroneous beliefs that we've integrated as truths. As a result of this, we're imprisoned by thoughts that are limiting and restricting.

"Man's main task is to give birth to himself,
to become
what he potentially is."
— *Erich Fromm*

I want to share with you an interesting *ah-ha!* that I had many years ago.

As a chiropractor, I'd often be asked, "Won't you get arthritis of your spine if it keeps being cracked like that?" The assumption was that cracking your knuckles would lead to osteoarthritic problems of the hand. Well, nothing is farther from the truth. (Oh, you too thought this was like the eleventh commandment?) You see, this is but one of hundreds of erroneous beliefs that we took as fact. It got me asking myself what other ideas I fostered that are equally inaccurate and how they served me. Since life is about looking through the windshield and not the rearview mirror, what have you learned from just this page alone?

Change will only take place by moving out of the groove. Nobody lifts the needle but us. It may be weird and difficult to be placed down in a new groove with a new song playing, but we'll never know if we don't risk. It's about embracing uncertainty, because within uncertainty lies all possibility!

Read and reread this, again and again. We live in a world where most of us need to know to be sure, to be certain. The reality is that we don't know if we'll be on this Earth tomorrow. So, Mr. or Mrs. Director of Your Life, how would you change your script? What scenery would you place behind the characters? What role would you select for yourself? What characteristics would you possess? Where would you turn up the volume and where would you lower it? You see, all of us have traits that empower or disempower us. All of us have everything that everyone else has. We're kind, evil, sinister, sarcastic, judgmental, bitter, and loving. The key is the volume, and the appropriateness of when the qualities manifest.

It would be unfair to conclude this chapter without a discussion of the "co-creator" of your life.

Life is much like a sailboat in the ocean. Follow me on this. We're not free from the tides, the winds, the currents, or the fury of nature. However, we're always able to set the sail and to hold the rudder. Simply stated, life's events are all the externals that often play havoc in our lives. Yet a sailor can "set his sail" to catch the wind, regardless of its direction, and can guide the direction of the boat as long as the other hand holds tight to the rudder.

This example may sound great in theory, but you're probably saying, "But you don't understand my circumstances!"

Although each of us could write a litany covering the enormity of our struggles, we still have the capacity to set the direction and harness the external forces to achieve our final destination.

I'll repeat myself, in the hope that you get this message, because if this is the only concept you walk away from this entire book, it will be worth its weight in gold.

"You can't control your circumstances, but you can control how you react!"

It's never the events, it's our interpretation!

I've learned how powerful this message is on many occasions in my life. What I'm grateful for is having and owning this wisdom in advance of my crises.

In 1982, my wife gave birth to our first child. The joy, happiness, and elation were overwhelming. By the sixth month, it was apparent that our little boy was having difficulty with his right hand and arm. As a chiropractor, I was sensing concerns on a much bigger scale, based on Jason's symptoms. We chose to take Jason to a pediatrician for an assessment. The doctor evaluated our little boy and was suspicious that he had a hemiparesis (a condition whereby one side of the body lacks normal control). This condition is caused by a stroke, either in utero or during the birthing process. Needless to say, for any parent, never mind first-time parents, it was a shock. What would this mean? Would he be able to use that side of his body? Would he be able to play sports? Would he be an outcast among his peers? You know the process I was going through.

We finally saw the head of neurology at Columbia Presbyterian Hospital in NYC, and on that day, it was confirmed that "your child had a stroke!"

As I close my eyes and try to feel what I felt at that moment, I shutter with a sense of helplessness, lassitude, and grief. I defaulted to my weakness rather than standing up to my greatness!

Don't let go of that last statement, because I've learned that we often default to society's software! We, in that moment, exercise the language, the pain, the sounds, and the pressures of all we saw when people were shocked, dismayed, or momentarily crippled by an event or circumstance.

Fortunately, I'd been fascinated by the subject of self-help psychology. Five years prior to Jason's birth, I had the good fortune of attending a seminar just after graduating from chiropractic college. It was during that weekend when I got the *ah-ha!*—a need that would serve me for the rest of my life. Allow me to shorten a weekend of information, knowledge, and wisdom into a simple sentence.

"The most important space is the space between your ears!"

It's not your circumstances in life, but your interpretation of those circumstances that's important. Do you get this? Don't read further until you clearly understand the depth and the value of owning this concept. It alone will carry you through the predictable, varied and many "speed bumps" of life!

Write down two major events or challenges that you've had in your lifetime. How did you react? Did you default to society's way of seeing it and have a pity party or did you use them as stepping-stones to move closer to your dreams?

Write down what your authentic self did at that moment. Did you go unconscious and live out what you had heard from your mother, father, teacher, or preacher?

What could you have said? What alternative view could you have taken if you had clearly understood the concept above?

Remember this for the rest of your life! We're not free from biology, nature, instincts, or genetics, nor are we free from the malfunctioning of our brains or bodies (illness or congenital defects), but we are free to interpret how they can serve us! We *choose* our response to the fateful events of our lives.

Having spent years understanding this philosophy, I endeavored to wipe back my tears and ask a better question.

What could I do and what seeds could I plant in my young child so he would never understand the concept of *can't*?

That was the beginning of turning obstacles into stepping-stones, of eliminating doubt, and of embracing an *"I can"* attitude!

I made a pledge to myself that nothing would take a higher level of importance than assisting my son in reaching his full potential. I wanted him to do whatever any other child of his age could do, regardless of the skill level—just to actively participate and never to hear the words *"You can't!"*

I urge you to read Shad Helmstetter's book, *What to Say When You Talk to Yourself!* It's appropriate to suggest this at this point, because the author denotes the extreme negative programming most of us have received. Helmstetter comments that "during the first eighteen years of our lives, you were told 'NO' or what you could not do more than 148,000 times. The occasional words of belief were just that, occasional, and they were far outweighed by our daily doses of 'cannots!'"

It's my hope and prayer that this book sets you on your journey. You deserve to introspect and see what foundation you were reared with. What principles were laid down early in your life to create your vision of yourself and your potential?

Can you see at this point that we're rarely the producer and directors of our lives? It's a program loaded into our initial hard drives that brought us to where we are!

Think about that! You are not *you*!

You're someone else's software package until you raise

your conscious awareness and challenge your own beliefs about your abilities, your choices, your reactions, and your interpretation of events.

Do you find this empowering? I hope so. Just the awareness that you can, in a moment, make a decision to change the meaning you give to anything! Whose meaning have you been giving to your life up until now?

The intent of this work is simply to plant seeds. I want you to go "silent" every day for a set period of time. The purpose of this is to get in touch with your soul. Your essence is your inner voice, that unique human being who is desperately trying to break out of the shackles of someone else's creation. Your mission is to find the authentic you.

Oftentimes, we're excited about doing this, but immediately default to excuses! It takes too much time, too much work, or it's too depressing to work on this.

The question I raise is: How painful will it be to be lying on your death bed, quietly stating what your voice wanted you to do over all those years? What will be your *coulda's, woulda's, shoulda's,* or *someday I'lls?*

Wow! What does all this mean? I believe that raising our level of conscious awareness is a prerequisite for experiencing a life worth living. Without consciousness, we remain in a state of "I didn't know that I didn't know!"

I want for you the same that I want for myself. I want to be the authentic author of my life. I want to produce and direct my life, in accordance with **my heart.** I say my heart, because I've learned that it's there that my correct guidance system resides. The heart is pure, untainted, and unadulterated. The challenge, once again, is not to allow the domineering effect of society's cultural software to drown out the subtle, yet pure, whispers of your heart.

I find it fascinating that after consuming hundreds of books, there lies at the very foundation of all of them a common thread that conveys the same message: we must silence ourselves daily! Like a pristine lake in the mountains, only with stillness is there reflection. Authors, after thousands of years, can't be wrong. It's us who need to be mindful of their wisdom.

Reduce the noise. Turn down the volume of Life and Doing! Remind yourself of who you are. You're a Human *Being*, not a Human *Doing*!

§

Chapter 4

Wisdom
in Advance of Crisis

How often in our lives have we looked in the proverbial rearview mirror in order to better understand the events that have taken place? How fortunate I am to have had exposure to the laws of attitude and success consciousness. Upon graduating from New York Chiropractic College, I participated in a seminar to help us prepare for life outside the classroom. Although there were clinical courses available, I found myself gravitating to the programs dealing with what I call "the space between your ears." I was blessed to have met a number of mentors who helped guide me in a more spiritual direction.

It's been said many times before that it's easy to ride the crest of success when all is going right. However, we determine the true character of a person during times of adversity. It's imperative for all of us to embrace the concept of humility. If you've lived long enough, you too know that the circumstances of your life don't always go in your favor. Remember, it's not your circumstances. It's your interpretation of the circumstances. It's not what happens. It's how you react to those events.

In my journey to investigate what makes successful people tick, I remember reading a story about the power of the subconscious mind. The author explained how our mind at birth is like a blank blackboard. It's a fertile garden, simply in need of seeds to be planted. We become that which we think about most of the time. We are what our environment is. The subconscious mind is our servant and will believe whatever it hears most often. So many of these concepts were quietly repeating themselves over and over in my head, day in and day out.

It became apparent to me that my son's illness was a perfect opportunity to see how effective these principles could work in a real-life situation. From that day forward, I'd put my son to sleep in his crib and kneel down beside him. As I quietly stroked his silky blond hair and forehead, I'd repeat over and over how much love I had for him and how there was no such thing as the word *can't*.

That was a daily event. It was my intention to help create a belief system in my son's subconscious mind that would constantly remind him that everything was possible.

It was recommended that we take Jason to physical therapy in order to support his right arm and right leg. After my first visit to the facility, I knew in my heart that it was not the environment he needed for a successful recovery. There were children who had such severe neurological damage and

I didn't want Jason to interpret his problem as being that severe.

I've learned through the wisdom of books, tapes, and seminars that what we see, smell, taste, and simply experience becomes part of our reality. It's called our *ambient environment*. This concept is very powerful, because many of us don't realize that our children are picking up the totality of the experience, whether in the classroom or at home.

There's much more than just the words we use that registers in our minds and in our hearts. In fact, in the world of human communication, it's estimated that only seven percent of what we get from one another are words. Thirty-three percent is gained from the tonality, and fifty-five percent from our physiology—our facial expressions, gestures, and the movement of our eyes. One can easily say that we must pay much attention to things beyond the spoken word if we're going to have quality relationships with one another, and certainly with our children. Most of us are blind to our own actions. We don't see ourselves, and all too often we're even unconscious in terms of what we say.

> "No act of kindness,
> no matter how small, is ever wasted."
> —*Aesop*

The story continues concerning Jason and the benefits, along with the challenges, of his stroke. I've learned so much about the incredible capability of the human body. When Jason was one and a half, late in the evening, I walked into our home to a sight that sent ice through my veins. Out of nowhere, Jason began seizing. He was as limp as a dishrag. His eyes rolled back and he was frothing from the mouth. His right arm was like a metronome, repeatedly contracting in a consistent pattern. Within moments, every system of his body went limp. He urinated and defecated as his nervous system short-circuited.

We rushed Jason to the emergency room of our local hospital, where he was administered Valium to quiet his out-of-control nervous system. It was one of the most frightening evenings of my life as my wife and I held hands, hoping and praying that he'd know who we were upon awakening—if, in fact, he'd awaken at all. Would he know his name? Would there be any brain damage? My mind raced out of control with fear, agitation, and the realization of how helpless we really are when it comes to the frailty of the human body. Despite the calamity and the feeling of helplessness, there was a very deep residing belief in me that "this too shall pass," and that Jason's body would endure the uncontrollable event.

Needless to say, after a sleepless night at the hospital, Jason did come around and slowly demonstrated normal physical and neurological function. Over the next four years, Jason had a seizure each year of a similar magnitude and we all endured the event each time. After consulting with the head of neurology at Columbia Presbyterian Hospital, it was advised that Jason would require medication to control the seizures, and that he'd need them for the rest of his life.

I went through the arduous task of calculating the number of minutes over the course of four years that Jason was actually in a state of seizure. It seemed unfair to have to medicate him (or any child) when those events occurred with a frequency of less than .00000004 percent of his life. Yet I understood that there could be life-threatening situations if he had a sudden seizure while swimming, riding a bicycle, or some other event, leading to a horrible accident. It's in these moments that we need to go into our hearts more than our minds to make decisions. My heart wanted to investigate other options rather than having to medicate my child for the rest of his life. However, due to pending fear, legitimate as it was, I defaulted to the doctor's demands and Jason was put on an anti-seizure drug.

The plot thickens.

In approximately four weeks, we needed to bring Jason for a blood work-up. Within hours, I received a frantic phone call at my office, telling me to immediately discontinue all medication. A blood test had showed that Jason was developing aplastic anemia. For the layman, this is a fatal disease in which the body stops producing red blood cells—a rare side effect of that specific medication.

It's essential that I share this story with you, because it eloquently and metaphorically explains the concept of why we should listen to our hearts more than our heads. Although you may not have had experiences like this to date, it is simply a matter of time. **None of us escapes *Life 101*!**

Over time, I was able to find the services of a chiropractor who worked specifically with the cranium (skull). Fifteen to eighteen visits were made to this practitioner over a period of four or five months. To this day, nobody can explain what ultimately occurred inside the nervous system of my son. I simply remain in a state of humility and gratitude, recognizing the incredible power of the human body to self-correct and self-regulate. As I write this book, Jason is twenty-four years old, hasn't had a seizure in more than twenty years, and takes no medication.

It's been said that there are countless billions of cells, acting, reacting, and interacting in a fantastic concert of highly intelligent activity, of which no doctor or group of doctors knows more than a fragment. The mystery of life is still a mystery. I ask you to expand your current belief system and embrace your body's ability to find harmony and balance.

I wish I could tell you that this was the end of the story regarding Jason and his health challenges. A bunch of years went by and we watched an amazing young man adapt to the requirements of playing soccer, basketball, and baseball. In fact, although Jason played baseball with only one arm, he made the all-star team in three of the four years he played. Remember the concept of success consciousness? There's always a way! As I reflect back on how I originally defaulted to the poor little unfortunate me and how I wouldn't have the pleasure of watching my little boy enjoy Little League, I clearly understand the power of that limited software package given to most of us, preventing humanity from embracing what's possible and seeing the potential everywhere.

Now we fast-forward the story to the summer of 1995. Jason was away at summer camp, like so many other teenagers were when school ended. It was approximately 4:30 a.m. when the phone rang at our home. A phone call at that time of the morning never feels good. I didn't recognize the voice on the other end, but it was calm, with a touch of urgency. This gentleman told me that Jason had just come down from upstairs, but he seemed disoriented and was complaining of abdominal pain. I asked if Jason could come to the phone. A moment later, I heard a feeble voice, attempting to articulate what he was feeling.

I asked my son to put the man back on the phone and instructed him to call 911, just in case there was something more than just severe abdominal cramping. I explained to the gentleman that I was going to get dressed, get into my car, and drive down to Philadelphia to pick Jason up and bring him home so we could have our doctor take a closer look and see what was going on.

Approximately two hours later, I received a phone call in my car, telling me to meet them at the local hospital where they were taking Jason for an evaluation. Shortly thereafter, we entered the emergency room and were greeted by a physician, who escorted us to where Jason was resting. As we walked into this room, there was my son, with wires and leads all over his body.

"Your son has been diagnosed with juvenile diabetes."

Another defining moment when life makes you question why. My mind was racing. Diabetes? How can that be? He'd never had problems like that. Nobody in my family had that problem.

So, after more tears, heartache, and asking god, "What more do you want from this boy?" we began the process of acceptance. It was mandated that we stay in the hospital for five days, learning all of the intricacies necessary to help support a child with juvenile diabetes.

This chapter is about wisdom. I learned a long time ago to **accept what is**. It's not always the easy thing to do, but it is the only thing to do. To complicate matters, my mother, four days prior to us finding out about Jason and his diabetes, was suddenly diagnosed with pancreatic and liver cancer. (This was beginning to sound like the old *Queen for a Day* show that aired on TV, approximately forty years ago. The winner was the person with the most misery in her life.) Well, at that moment, I certainly felt like I was the winner, because things had never been that bad for me personally.

Once the emotions settled, I asked myself to draw from all the reading, tapes, books, and seminars I'd attended over the years. I became mindful. I recognized that we can't undo the events and circumstances that life deals us. What we can and must do is be proactive, take action, and ask how these events will serve us.

I remember specifically talking with Jason and explaining to him how much he was loved by his family and friends, but the disease was his disease, and how he chose to take care of himself would be the distinguishing factor for its outcome.

Then I said, "Let's get to work."

Personally, I was feeling a bit stronger once we came home from the hospital. The name of the game with any health care concern is management. Jason's endocrinologist told him how important it was to monitor his blood sugar. He explained that if Jason chose not to, eventually he could lose his limbs to amputation and go blind. Those were powerful words and provoked some serious concerns. With a background in exercise physiology, and my training as a chiropractor, I knew how important exercise would be for Jason in the management and control of his diabetes. Weight training would also improve his muscle tone and facilitate fine motor coordination.

A decision was made. We converted the children's playroom into a beautiful gym, housing weights and aerobic equipment. In less than one year, Jason saw enormous changes, both in his physical structure as well as in the management of his blood sugar numbers. His endocrinologist was so impressed that he called me to tell me that in his thirty-five years of working with diabetic children he had never seen a child so in control of their blood sugar.

The essence of the chapter is wisdom, philosophy, and seeing how everything and every circumstance can ultimately serve us. I wrote a letter to Muscle and Fitness magazine and shared Jason's story. We were asked to come to Columbus, Ohio, to meet with the editor of *Muscle and Fitness*. It was an incredible weekend. Not only was Jason interviewed, but we also had the good fortune of meeting Arnold Schwarzenegger. A few months later, in the January 1999 edition of *Muscle and Fitness*, a two-page article, entitled "Turning Obstacles into Opportunities: How a young diabetic took a life challenge to a whole new level" was published.

The message I want to drive home is that it isn't what happens to us but, once again, how we interpret the events. All I wanted was for Jason to care for himself, to love himself enough to want to do whatever it took to stay well. All of those events supported his self-image, which is the key for all of us on this planet. The universal complaint, cross culturally and around the world, is **"I'm not enough"** (smart, tall, skinny, intelligent, rich, or whatever).

I was taught that the best way of learning something was to teach it. Since Jason was doing such a phenomenal job in managing his blood sugar numbers, why not share that knowledge with other juvenile diabetic children? That's all Jason needed to hear. Within one week, he was registered to be a certified personal trainer. At fifteen years of age, he was the youngest attendee in the program.

"Persistence and determination alone are omnipotent."

This quote is powerful. When Jason suffered his stroke, the broca area of the brain was affected. This is the learning center. The final examination for personal training was an in-depth, all-encompassing examination, dealing with anatomy, physiology, and the basic laws of physics. Jason passed the practical examination and missed a passing grade on the written section by only four points. I bring this up because there is no such thing as failure. Just because we don't succeed in the first go around, there's no reason not to persist when we want something bad enough. We must DWIT (do whatever it takes)! That was a lesson Jason needed to know. That's a lesson for all of us to learn and practice. Disappointments are commonplace. We must endure, stay focused, and simply continue until we reach our target.

Last, but not least, in this incredible journey, at the ripe old age of fifteen and a half , Jason started his own home-based business, training juvenile diabetic children. I constructed a letter and mailed it to my patient base.

It asked those who received it, "Who do you know who has children with diabetes?"

I explained what Jason's dream was and within two weeks, he had ten full-time clients. Jason saw children in our home, before school began and after school ended.

My greatest joy came when one mother took me aside and said, "The best thing that ever happened in my life was having your son enter my child's life."

Nothing more need be said.

So, what can you take from this chapter? It doesn't take a special person to make these things happen. It takes philosophies to help us make choices. What perceptions do we have of ourselves and of our children? Love, support, and a conscious effort to nurture their feelings of self are paramount in rearing our offspring. Lastly, **BE** the person you are hoping your children will become—make fewer demands and be more congruent with your words and actions.

Write down two major events or challenges that you've had in your lifetime. Did you default to society's way of seeing it? Did you have a pity party for yourself?

Write down what your authentic self did at that moment. Did you go unconscious and live out what you heard from your mother, father, teacher, or preacher?

What could you had said? What alternative could you have taken if you had clearly understood the concept of "it's not your circumstances in life, but rather your interpretation of these circumstances?"

§

"For we in this generation, and in the United States are the pampered of our planet...we are the fat of the land. Never in history, nowhere else in the world have such numbers of human beings eaten so much, exerted themselves so little, and become and remained so fat. We have come suddenly into the land of milk and honey and we look at, and we suffer because of it."

—*Jean Mayer*

Chapter 5

God's Miracle Pill

Although man's technology has advanced greatly, the needs of the human body have not changed since the beginning of time. Man was put on this planet to be a hunter and gatherer. Muscles are meant to be used. When they're not, they'll deteriorate. If you succumb to the philosophy of easy living, you must then pay the price in decreased efficiency.

Too often people mistakenly contend that physical activity is for the athlete or super fit person. They believe that unfit persons, leading sedentary lives, should refrain from exercise. Nothing can be further from the truth. All human beings have a blueprint for fitness and physical prowess. This is called *heredity*. We all begin life with a functional potential that sets particular limits for health and physical fitness. However, even a poor genetic endowment doesn't imply that one should be fatalistic and regard any effort to enhance fitness as futile.

There's no justification for discontinuing physical activity on the grounds that benefits derived in the past will carry over to the future. The body deconditions itself quicker than it takes to reach the level of fitness desired. Exercise must be continued and be progressive for any benefits to be derived.

The intent of this chapter isn't to be redundant with simply more information on the value of exercise, but more importantly, to assist you in genuinely identifying and resonating with the importance of exercise in your life. It's imperative that you answer the following questions:

1. If I continue my current exercise habits and patterns, where will I be five years from now?

2. What kind of model am I for my children to follow? (Because follow, they will!)

3. How congruent are my intention with my exercise habits? In other words, we desire a strong, toned and confident body, but our daily actions rarely support this vision.

4. If I don't feel accepting of how I look, how will lack of exercise improve this condition?

Take a few minutes to review these questions, and if you're really motivated, answer them honestly and completely. The greatest value we can get from any book, magazine, or periodical is to focus on the few powerful concepts that somehow touch us at our *heart level*. Reading alone will do nothing to move us physically. However, the space between the words, what we're feeling, will be the impetus to get us to do that which we know we need to do, and that's the very essence of this chapter.

I don't care if you remember any of the facts and figures, statistics, or general information I've shared. What's important is that something reaches you on a heartfelt level that makes you decide to commit because you want to commit.

Remember, "Without the WHY, there's no comply." You want to achieve the goal of a strong, toned, and confident body that each of us truly desires. Ultimately, please remember, you're the captain of your ship, the master of your own destiny. **"If it's to be, it's up to me."** This isn't psychobabble. This is the way it works here on planet Earth. Stop finger-pointing, blaming, and feeling sorry for yourself. Life is a do-it-to-yourself process. The very first step in this process of transformation of who we are and who we want to be begins with an open and honest self-inventory of where we are now! If you're comfortable with this place now, do nothing about it. However, please be honest enough to acknowledge that a change is necessary. Taking that step is empowering, and I honor you for being honest with yourself.

Physiological effects

Exercising aerobically (running, jogging, swimming, or bicycling) is any exercise that taxes your oxygen-transporting systems (heart and lungs). Such exercises will increase the strength and efficiency of the muscles surrounding the lungs, assisting in opening more usable lung space and ultimately increasing the total lung capacity.

Aerobic exercise increases tissue vascularization (increasing the number of tiny blood vessels surrounding the muscle tissue). The consequence of this **collateral circulation** is increased avenues for the blood to bathe the active tissue. More importantly, if a blockage should occur as a result of an embolism in one vessel, the body now has alternative routes for the life-supporting material to travel. Exercise helps create a **built-in emergency care unit** that one day may save your life.

Exercise seems to have several beneficial effects on the metabolism of cholesterol and triglycerides (the major blood fats). Since the fat molecule can be broken down for fuel consumption, exercise can inhibit and reduce its concentration in the blood. Exercise is a wonderful cathartic. It assists the muscles of digestion in eliminating wastes and consequently increases bowel activity. Initiating and following through with an exercise program could prevent chronic constipation, which plagues the majority of the elderly population. Clearly, the physiological benefits of regular aerobic exercise are endless. The goal of any exercise program should be to lower the heart rate while increasing the strength of its contraction (stroke volume). A heart working under the above circumstances would be a more efficient engine, assuming that all else is normal.

As I mention often in both my seminars, it's less important that you have an enormous understanding of the physiology of exercise. What's most important is that you recognize how crucial the role of participating in an exercise program is for you now and most importantly, for the quality of your life going forward.

I love the following quote: "Those who think they have no time for bodily exercises will, sooner or later, have to find time for chronic illness."

I find it fascinating to take a close look at our lives. Most of us operate on an extensive system of erroneous beliefs and false hopes when it comes to the areas of exercise and nutrition. We're so unconscious of what's going on at a deeper level that we blame lack of time or lack of interest on our poor eating habits and pathetic exercise regimen. It's also easy to blame a society that urges us to eat large amounts of poor quality foods. The advertising industry works feverishly to associate high profile celebrity personalities with their particular food. They understand the incredibly frail ego that most of us have and recognize our buying habits as a result.

Technology is clearly a two-edged sword. On one hand, the electronics industry has created incredible opportunities to make our lives, communication systems, and business systems more efficient. Yet they've created games and computers that have kept our youth indoors, stagnant, and with limited motion. Simply look at the obesity crisis. It's been estimated at close to forty percent of American youth will be clinically obese by their early teens. If obesity is a predisposition for diabetes, hypertension, and heart disease, what is the future of America?

As I'm writing this text, one of the greatest challenges our country is facing, besides security and terrorism, is the crisis of our health care system. I'll forgo the exact statistics, but we read every day about how difficult it is for American businesses to stay profitable due to the exorbitant cost of health insurance for its workers. There is a clear message I'll make in this chapter. It's simply this:

Each of us must take personal responsibility for our own health going forward. This isn't just a good idea, it's the only answer for longevity and quality of life, individually, as well as a way to preserve the future of our nation.

The real challenges I see to taking personal responsibility are the following:

1. Challenge your belief systems. Do you seriously believe that you can eat anything you want, stay totally inactive, and think that if you get sick the American health care system will simply give you the appropriate pill or medication to correct your maladies? I sincerely believe that many people resonate with the concept that medical advances are so powerful that doctors and hospitals can undo the ill health brought about by poor lifestyle choices.

2. We live in a culture where there are more doctors per capita, more hospitals available to its people, and yet we rank poorly compared to many other countries around the world. How do we explain that? Individually, we must **place attention on our good intentions**. We all want good health and longevity for ourselves and our family members. However, if each of us takes **an open, honest inventory of our daily actions and habits**, we'll see how blatantly incongruent we are. Our lack of activity, our sedentary nature, combined with poor food choices, will **never get us to our intention of good health in our future years**.

3. Only through conscious awareness can any of us maintain the habits and actions that are crucial to the attainment of these goals. So

what is conscious awareness? It's simply to **be in the moment**! Wow, have you ever heard that concept before? Of course you have, but do you realize how difficult it really is? With our lives as complex and busy as they are for most of us, it's inordinately challenging to really live with that kind of focus. Allow me, at this point, to make some recommendations that have worked well for me.

• **The power of planning.** The only way for us to make changes in all our lives going forward is to get clear on all the ways we are self-sabotaging our health and well-being. We've got to carve out a time slot for the respective days that we plan on doing our physical activity. This is very important. However, even more significant is **finding your why**. Why do it? Why bother? Why make it part of your week? These questions must be answered by you! **Nobody else's answer is important**. It will not sustain you or give you the fortitude going forward. To make this a significant enough event, you have to participate for the rest of your life. The operative words here are **the rest of your life**. Please understand that the true value of exercise will only show up in your life if it is sustained. Periodic exercise is certainly better than sedentary behavior, but it will never provide you with the benefits and the physical changes that it creates in the human body when sustained over time.

- **Loving oneself.** What I am referring to here is not ego love. I want to believe that each of us cares enough about ourselves and our future health care that we will make choices that serve us rather than harm us. Once again, the obvious, honest assessment I was asking you to do earlier will be your metaphoric mirror. Take a look at your current actions and habits. How do they support your quest for a strong body with reserved energy to handle the challenges of each day?

There's an expression that states: **"We have within us everything we need to know whenever we need to know it."** Therefore, it's not more facts we need, but a healthier understanding of who we are and what's making us take these poor action steps, leading to unhealthy futures.

So I ask you to take a blank piece of paper and write out what allows you to make choices that self-sabotage your goals, your aspirations, and your self-love. Remember, without handling these questions, you'll simply perpetuate the same behavior that led you exactly to where you are today. If that's satisfactory for you, please continue with those choices and behaviors. However, if you're tired of carrying excessive weight and willing to recognize that your choices are making your heart work harder, then it's time for change—and **that change is now.**

Your past doesn't equate to your future. Our futures begin

at any given moment. **Without the why, there's no comply!** Do you get this? Do you understand the significance of this one action step? I hope you do, and I hope this exercise touches you on an emotional level. It's always those things that touch our heart strings that cause us to take necessary action in our lives. I'm writing this material not to police anyone or to tell you how to live your life. What I'm hoping to do is help you make the necessary shifts that will bring more happiness, more serenity, and finally, more peace into your life. There's no greater blessing than to simply be OK with who you are.

When we live each day, taking good care of our physical and emotional health, the countless billions of cells that are running our bodies would say, if they could, "Thank you for caring about me."

Lastly, in my estimation, one of the most important activities that must be carried out daily (with daily being the operative word) is to confront every morning with the following question: "What will I do today that will move me toward my physical goals?" It's only this type of spaced repetition that will allow us to stay focused in a sea of distraction. Only five to ten minutes every morning will center you and allow you to live the day with strong intention.

§

"We must all suffer from one of two pains—
the pain of discipline or the pain of regret.
The difference is discipline weighs ounces,
while regret weighs tons."

Chapter 6

Create A Day,
Master Your Life

One of the most valuable lessons I've been taught is the concept of chunking things down. Nothing can be more overwhelming than to confront all of what life challenges us with. However, if we apply the concept of breaking something large into its simplest components, why can't we do that with our life? Why not take an individual day, in fact, today, the only day we ever have, and make it a masterpiece?

As an artist, if your canvas was your day and you held a pallet of colors in your hand, what would you paint? I've thought about this question many times. If I could orchestrate a day, I'd be certain to include activities that involve exercise, nutrition, spirituality, and my work. The components of exercise and nutrition, in my estimation, are mandatory, because without our physical health, nothing else matters. This is a point I want to drive home in every chapter of this book. We need to be reminded often because our "software" is programmed to focus more on the needs outside of us. The drug of society is as powerful as the gravitational pull of the Earth. Every day, in every way, our media centric society is pulling us to consume, spend, purchase, and change our **external being** in order for us to be OK. I'm fascinated as I scroll through the pages of magazines and newspapers to see the advertising and the effort placed on getting us to buy products in order to make us look or smell better or to be more attractive to the rest of the world.

Exercise

While many of us recognize the importance of exercise in our life, we simply don't participate. **To know and not to do is really not to know**. I love that expression because it so exemplifies our personalities. That is, if we know something, we interpret it as though we do it! Is that a fair statement? It's what I've observed as a doctor over the past thirty years of my practice.

Where you fit this exercise component in your day isn't the issue. It's the idea that it shows up somewhere. I want to make it clear that the kind of activity you choose becomes less of a concern. Just put your body in motion, raising your heart rate to at least 120 beats per minute and sustaining it for at least twenty minutes. If you're honest with yourself, you will see that a 20–30 minute "window" exists in all of our lives. It's been said that most of us spend more time planning a vacation than we do planning our lives! Can you relate to that?

> "One discipline always leads to another discipline."

Having worked with more than 7000 people, I've witnessed the devastating effects of deconditioning. This is what happens to the body as a result of sedentary lifestyles. It's been estimated that some eighty percent of all the chronic diseases we suffer from as a society are really lifestyle illnesses. What will it take for you to begin to make exercise part of your day? Will it be a cardiovascular disaster, stroke, Type 2 diabetes, or hypertension?

The essence of this component is to make you more **MINDFUL**. Conscious awareness, as I've stated often in this book, is the first step toward transformation. My intent in every chapter will be to challenge your belief systems and to have you take a personal inventory of your day. If you don't, you'll continue your destructive habits that have become so routine, that you don't even know you have. Is this not true?

In our sedentary world, where even our children are spending more time sitting with their menagerie of electronic games, there has never been a more important time to awaken to these destructive habits and commit to putting our bodies in motion.

Fast Forward. This is a term I like, because it allows us to visualize where we'll be ten years from now. Based on how you move, your current flexibility, and your level of morning stiffness, how functional will you be in ten years? Will you be able to get down on the floor with your grandchildren? Will you be able to ride a bike, play golf, or take a trip to that beautiful destination when you finally have the time and money? I'm simply providing you with the feedback I hear every day in my practice.

I'm writing this book with the goal that it helps to motivate others to **"get 'er done"** and to take the action we desperately need to if we're serious about **growing older gracefully**.

As we leave this section on exercise, give consideration to **what you're willing to DO**. Are you going to commit to it and finally make it part of your daily ritual going forward? Of course, there will be circumstances and events that make it impossible to do it every single day. The point is that there is never enough time for everything, but always enough time for the important things. Your responsibility, here and now, is to take a look at your values. Simply ask yourself what gets done. People who have aesthetics as high values are certain to have their hair and nails always handled. Why? Because it's a high priority. Spend a few minutes assessing your values and see if your values are congruent with what you want out of your life. It's a powerful experience to do this. Most of us want great health going forward. We want to be secure in our financial future. Yet when we confront our values and our daily actions and habits, we are often met with horrible incongruities, (such as financial security with no forced saving plan or great energy and vibrant health without an exercise plan in place). Awakening to this realization is a powerful moment. Do not go to the next part of this chapter without doing this simple, yet critical, self-assessment.

Nutrition

This section isn't about a dietary plan. It's once again an act of consciousness. I'm asking you to become **MINDFUL** of your food choices. What works well from a healthy eating plan is to put together foods you plan to eat in advance of your day. When I began to take personal responsibility for my food choices, I ate better foods more often.

I began to ask the questions, "How will I feel after eating this food?" and "How will this food look on me?"

Mindful questions allowed me to make better choices. It seems simple, and it really is if you are serious about looking and feeling good. The power is in the questions. All day long, you're making choices, minute by minute. Although you may not speak aloud, you're asking yourself questions on **EVERYTHING**!

Here's what I want you to walk away with from this chapter. Food affects every cell in your body. It's broken down to its molecules and impacts your mind to your skin, your emotions to your energy. Every morsel of food has the power to build or destroy our bodies, not at that moment, but over time. This is a very important point. Since what we eat doesn't manifest a problem immediately, we tend not to give it much thought. Then again, a cigarette doesn't have an immediate effect, either. My intention is to help you appreciate that good quality food will do much more than satisfy your immediate gratification of hunger. Each meal will lay the groundwork for hormones to be made and released, and simply to do their job as effectively as they can. Certain foods trigger specific hormones that either build or destroy our bodies.

"Never eat more than you can lift."
— *Miss Piggy*

Although it's not the purpose of this book to be a reference for nutritional facts and theories, it's worth mentioning the following:

There are **Four Pillars to Aging**, according to experts. (Read Barry Sears' *The Zone Diet*.)

1. **Excess insulin.** This happens as a result of our choosing to eat sugar. The increased glucose in the body is met with an insulin surge. Therefore, to keep this as elementary as possible, MINIMIZE the amount of sugar and refined white flour products. **Remember, excess insulin makes you fat and keeps you fat!**

2. **Excess cortisol.** Cortisol is an emergency hormone. It is what is sent out of our adrenal glands whenever the body is under a **STRESS** reaction. Severe anger, aggression, fear, anxiety, and other emotions will trigger cortisol release. What most people don't know is that dietary stress is induced by meals that contain large quantities of simple carbohydrates. As explained before, a rise in insulin is usually accompanied by a spike in cortisol.

3. **Excess blood sugar.** A tight control of blood sugar is mandatory for our bodies to work correctly. In order for the body to repair, regulate,

and regenerate itself, glucose levels must be at or near specific levels. We're fortunate that the body, through its own innate intelligence, can do this balancing act without our conscious awareness. However, when we overindulge in excessive simple sugars, our bodies react with cellular inflammation. To the average Joe, this means "silent inflammation." Just as the word implies, we have no clue that something isn't right. It's only after years of inflammation that the body shows symptoms of a problem. It's then given a diagnosis, yet there was **disease** brewing well before the onset of pain or problem. Bottom line: the closer we keep our blood sugar to a normal range, the more youthful our body will be. Nutrition is a key element in the game of anti-aging.

4. **Excess free radicals**. Simply stated, these are byproducts of a variety of stressors in the body. They include psychic stress, UV radiation, and oxidative stress from a high sugar diet. I cannot emphasize enough how important it is to avoid sugar in your diet. Every doughnut, candy bar, and soda adds to a toxic excess of dietary glucose.

So what does this mean to you? If aging gracefully is important in your life or the lives of your family members, it would behoove you to **take inventory of your lifestyle**. Remember, it is the **repeated actions, habits, and choices** we make everyday that collectively act to damage or to repair our cells on a deeper level of life than what we see every day. What I've realized after contemplating these contemplations is that the first twenty years of my life weren't very pretty on a cellular level. Those of us growing up in the '50s and '60s weren't privy to what we're aware of today. I was a scooter pie, French fry, Twinkie kind a guy from the Bronx, New York, and quite proud that I could muscle down 15–20 White Castle belly bombs, and then wash those babies down with a shake from Mister Softee at 10:30 on a summer night. Can you relate to this strict regimen of dietary excess?

For many of us, *reform* is the game! To at least come to a realization at some point in our life that change need be made is a positive first step. So your challenge, dear reader, is to make a choice **now**. Decide if some modifications are in order. Remember, my job isn't to police anyone, just to help awaken you from a stupor of poor habits. I honor you if you'll endeavor to heed these concerns. The bottom line is that, sooner rather than later, we'll sit down to a banquet of consequences and most of them aren't pretty.

Spirituality

When we participate in the honest and open inventory I've been speaking about, we ultimately ask the questions: Who am I? What is my purpose? What gifts have I brought to this world?

Our society has deeply programmed us to be focused on doing. However, **we're human *beings*, not human *doings*!** Maybe this explains why so many people continue to suffer with "anguish of the soul" despite their accomplishments, acquisitions, and arriving where they hoped to be. Have you witnessed the discontent that so many people refer to, despite having more than they've ever had in their lives?

I ask, "What's up with that?"

In my own authentic quest for meaning, here are some of my discoveries.

1. The greatest fulfillment in improving ourselves comes in our empowerment to more effectively reach out and help others.

2. Most of us know in our hearts that a bigger life is available to us, yet we're unsure about how to achieve it.

3. Create time for solitude. It's only when we quiet the mind that we can hear our heart. It's in the depth of our soul where the space unidentified by science as our true authenticity lies.

I love the line, "Our hearts are only twelve inches away from our heads, yet it can take a lifetime for the two to connect." My interpretation of this is as follows:

Our heads are the products of our mothers, fathers, teachers, and preachers. They laid the foundation for our belief systems, and, in essence, the meaning we have given to everything. Our hearts are pure. They resonate with our inner guidance system. The heart sings a song that has not been tainted by society. It represents your innate needs and desires. To hear it, however, you must go silent. For many of us in a world where we're measured by our productivity, we rarely allow ourselves the luxury of down time or quiet contemplation. If we aren't DOING something, we feel nonproductive, maybe even worthless. Imagine spending all of our time in someone else's plan for our lives! Well, if you've never taken the time to explore your own "voice," chances are you're living someone else's expectation of you. So round and round we go, buying more toys, adding to the plethora of "stuff" as we play the **"he who dies with the most toys wins" game**.

Can you relate to this interpretation of life? A bigger question to ask is: Is this YOU? I honor you if you said yes, because this may have been the first time you've seen yourself for who you really are. **A dictum in all consciousness raising programs states "one is powerless until one tells the truth."**

We began this program by creating a plan for the twenty-four hours we have in a day. I've worked hard to start every morning reading and writing for at least 10–15 minutes. The value of this work is to remind myself of my purpose by spending a few minutes in gratitude for all that I have in my life, not only the stuff, but the people, my children, my family, and my patients, who have provided me with a meaning for my existence.

I was taught through my reading that you can't be grateful and depressed at the same time. So please make a point of writing down five reasons you're grateful every morning. **Your energy goes where your mind flows.** If we don't direct our minds, they'll default to the negative. Have you ever experienced that? Of course you have—every morning, if you're like most people. Spiritual work is like other intensive pursuits, and can be arduous. It requires discipline, the development of tools, and unfailing concentration. It's my opinion that the quest for clarity about ourselves, our mission, and purpose is one worth pursuing.

Lastly, Steven Covey in his book, *The 8th Habit*, states the truth eloquently: "Our mission in life is to find our Voice and then to help others find theirs." Your voice is your dharma (purpose). Remind yourself every day of your value. Whenever you find yourself having a pity party for yourself, go and help someone. Watch how the act of kindness for someone other than yourself can change your emotions in a heartbeat.

Work

This four-letter word represents the last of the four components of our day. Here is where we'll spend approximately seventy percent of our lives. Have you ever realized it takes up that much time? Over the years, I've watched parents, and society at large, tell the next generation what to do relative to their employment. Before there was managed care, being a doctor had great connotations. A lawyer was and continues to be a highly desired goal. The purpose of this treatise on employment is to assist you in tweaking your authenticity. What is it that juices you? Are you living out someone else's goals and aspirations? There are too many people in the workforce who are doing just that. Never having "gone silent," they simply listened to the authorities of their lives and ventured into the domain of **other people's goals**.

For many of us, we can't easily move out of where we are. It isn't the purpose of this section to talk you out of your livelihood or in anyway insinuate that the work you're doing isn't what you like. As a health care professional, I've come to the understanding that our health and well-being is tied to what we do most of the time. More than half of our waking hours are spent on the job, and even more if we include commuting.

Once again, I ask, "How many people are enjoying what they do?"

The next question is, "Do you feel powerless to change this?"

We talk about nourishing ourselves with purpose and value, yet if we spend this amount of time every day, how can this be productive to our souls and to those around us? Here's what we discovered. No matter what food we're eating, if we dislike our job, it drains us emotionally and physically.

Joshua Rosenthal, in his book *Integrative Nutrition*, states, "Finding the work you love, loving the work you find." I love this phrasing because it's very difficult to just pick up and walk away from a career. An alternative is to really investigate areas within the work you are doing and ask better questions.

Years ago, I had a patient who commented, "Dr. Berg, you're so fortunate to have a job where you're really helping people. All I do is chase a f—g dollar."

I'll never forget that afternoon. Here was a man who was making a far better income than I, but who interpreted his work in a demeaning way. He was in the financial field, but saw himself chasing dollars rather than supporting people to create a more stable and secure financial future. My first recommendation is to reframe your own interpretation of your work. Find language that serves you and increases your own worth as a human being.

Lastly, ask the more important question. Where do you get lost in your own mind, where time stands still and you're thinking of nothing other than what you're absorbed in? Brainstorm that for ten minutes and then write down those activities that remind you of where your passion may lie.

It's been said before that most people live lives of quiet desperation. Most of us will never see the desperation of others, since we do a very effective job of hiding our honest feelings in a proverbial storage closet full of our shadows.

The intent of this chapter is to help all of us create utter visibility or better yet, transparency in our lives. What would your world be like if there was nothing to hide from? It would be hard to argue the fact that most people utilize clothing, cars, vacations, and most every other luxury item as a means to substantiate their own self-worth.

Every twenty-four hours represents an opportunity to embrace uncertainty. The "known" is nothing other than the prison of our past and all that we've been conditioned to. There's no evolution in that! Can you understand? Living each day as a carbon copy of the day before drowns each of us in a pool of stagnation, entropy, disorder, and decay. If you relate to this, it's time to jump out of the pool. Just feel what that feels like. I don't care how old you are, it's awful, and more importantly, it doesn't have to be like that. This entire book is about transformation. It can only happen once you recognize the nightmare in which you've been living. Better yet, be so appreciative as to climb out of the river of DENIAL and embrace a vision of something new that is possible. Are you with me?

There is reason to step into the unknown. It's the arena where **ALL IS POSSIBLE**, ever fresh and steaming with new manifestations. Remember this: Without uncertainty, life is just the stale repetition of worn-out memories. You become a victim of the past, and your torment of today is the proof. **READ THAT AGAIN.** Who do you know who lives that way—a family member, a good friend, or maybe *you*?

Contemplate your contemplations. What vision of possibility comes to you when you consider living your life differently? What has served me well over the years has been embracing philosophies that were different from those I was reared with. I want to give you a different vision. Remember what's been stated repeatedly throughout this book. We're like a record needle stuck in the groove of a vinyl record, unable to move forward, so round and round we go, unable to advance. When you do the work and consciously ask yourself what each of these concepts mean to you, you, and you alone, will have your answers. One thought conjures a stream of consciousness and you'll begin to come alive and experience personal growth. It is a powerful experience and it's my hope that this material will help you spawn new insights and distinctions.

Every day is, in fact, a stepping into uncertainty. Welcome it, because it's here that all possibility exists. Your future holds excitement, adventure, mystery, magic, and celebration. Remember that your past holds security and certainty, but no evolution. We want our lives to evolve into the masterpiece they were intended to be.

This is a good point to be reminded that we must challenge our past conditioning. We've been prisoners of our pre-programming! Today we're making conscious efforts to recognize this fact and do something to create a new program that bathes us in possibility and good energy. This isn't wishful thinking, but a daily habit of revisiting our spirit and becoming the most authentic people we can be. No more hiding, lying, or denying what is. That game becomes exhausting and futile over time.

Hang out with ideas vs. people

Think about this for a moment. You and I have come up

with some inspiring concepts. Because we're conditioned to doubt ourselves, we reach out to our family and friends, but for what? Validation! We question our own ideas, due to the inflicted negativity that our past provided for us.

Here's what I've come to believe is real. If we can create a concept, a dream, an inspiration, we can attain it. The purpose of this share is to remind you that **"we have within us everything we need to know, whenever we need to know it."**

I am asking you to once again contemplate your contemplations. What are you thinking about most of the time? I remember reading that most of us have a loop. That loop is a perpetual thought process that only deviates periodically throughout the day, as when we need to make momentary decisions. Beyond those, what is the dominant CONTEMPLATION that you spend most of your day with? **The next question is: why?**

This is a powerful exercise, because it allows you to do an internal audit of what has priority in your life. It's the thing that takes up much of your life energy and holds you back from allocating this energy toward the inspiration that could be central to your life—your voice, your dharma. Write down five of the most common occurring thought patterns that you hold onto every day.

I urge you to develop the habit of spending the first half hour of every day with yourself, your ideas, and your pen and paper. Remember, you can be part of the herd or **true to yourself**. It's been estimated that ninety-seven percent of the people in our country do what everybody else does, think the same thoughts, and collectively act out similar habits. Since the herd awakes late, grabs coffee on the run, and begins the day with an inflammatory lifestyle." CHOOSE to be like the other three percent. Awaken with an intention to spend a few valuable moments with the most important person in your life—**YOU.**

How do you want to live out this twenty-four hour period? What are your convictions about you?

The most valuable statement I can make here is that you RECOGNIZE that you have the ability to choose your contemplations, those thoughts you spend day in and out with. Just realizing this and having the conscious awareness to recognize that you're contemplating them is a huge step in this process of becoming aware.

Why have meditation, solitude, peace, and serenity been such popular words in our society over the last few years? Simply stated, these are the **states of being** that most of us want, yet have a hard time achieving. It's only in these quiet contemplative moments that we can hear our heart's voice.

Remember, we've been domesticated, programmed, and scripted to say, to act, and to do exactly as we always have. It's time for a quiet revolution within ourselves to break the shackles of living someone else's beliefs, ideals, dreams, and goals.

Only through daily contemplation can you unshackle your mind and unleash new, creative, honest self-talk that inspires, infuses, and moves you in the direction of your dreams. (RFY—right for you goals.)

Having spoken with thousands of people, I know how often we tend to move in the direction of **OPG (other people's goals)**. That's why it's critical to do the self-inventory and ask yourself EVERY MORNING what your intentions are and if they're moving you toward what's RIGHT FOR YOU.

Contemplate this contemplation: Are you OK to be with just you?

You may be asking, "What are you talking about?"

My experience in talking with so many people and getting insights to their worlds has made me understand how frightening it is to be alone with one's thoughts. It's one of the reasons why too many people spend their lives DOING, rather than BEING. You know the mantra, **we're human *beings*, not human *doings*,** yet more people are fixated on the doing side, spending no time just being. These same people find themselves with more stuff, more things, and all too often, still emotionally and spiritually bankrupt. Do you know anyone fitting this bill? Sound like something you can relate to?

Bottom line: spend more time with yourself, and less time talking to the naysayers of the world. Life is too short, and you and I need the support of those who can assist us and be the wind under our wings, not the weight on our tails.

§

"We are learning that our health is intimately woven with our mental outlook, emotional tone, and spiritual well being."

Chapter 7

Stupid Dora

I was fortunate enough to have had a grandmother who withstood the adversities of 103 years on this planet. Nanny, as she was affectionately called, was the true matriarch of our family. She traveled from the west side of the Bronx to the northeast corner of that borough every day to watch over my sister and me, allowing my mother to go off to work. Nanny didn't drive, so she walked to the subway, had to change trains, and finally waited for a bus to get her to our home each day. She reversed this commute and returned home to make dinner for her husband.

Some people would say, "Chuck, why on earth are you writing a chapter in your book about your grandmother? That's like asking a stranger to sit down next to you and watch your family movies."

My answer will be found by the time you complete these few pages.

It was 1995. My mom had just been buried after being

ravaged with pancreatic cancer. She was diagnosed on August 9th and died November 6, 2005, just twelve weeks from her day of diagnosis. To watch my grandmother suffer, observing her only remaining child wither away in the next room, was heart wrenching. She had lost her son in World War II while he fought the Germans on French soil in 1944, so grief had been part of her world for more than sixty years. The fear of losing her daughter to illness and of outliving both her children was a parent's proverbial worst nightmare.

OK, enough suffering—or is it? Fast forward—Dora (Nanny) was in the Hebrew Home for the Aged in Riverdale, New York. It was July of 2002. Like the story, *Tuesdays with Morrie*, mine was "Thursdays with Nanny." There was nobody left in her world. I made that day *our* day and would visit for an hour each week.

The fascinating part of our weekly visitations with my grandmother was to listen to what she shared. Remember, Dora was then 103. She had an enormity of life events that flashed across her long-term memory screen. She'd spend hours, as most seniors do in nursing homes, reflecting on her life, her disappointments, and her heartfelt moments.

Almost every visit would include the histrionics of her early years. Stop for a moment and ask yourself: what do you contemplate most of the time? When we contemplate our contemplations, we find that there really are only a few repetitive concerns that tend to dominate our minds most of the time. We all have a story.

Dora's mother had died of pneumonia when my grandmother was only seven. Her dad then remarried a woman who had very little patience for anyone, never mind **his children**. From the first day she came into my grandmother's life, she was demanding and demeaning. At age seven, Dora would come home from first grade and her job, before anything else, was to hand wash cloth diapers. Yes, that's right, excrement and all. Not exactly what you and I did when we got home from school! Just a little bit different than a scooter pie and a glass of milk. According to my grandmother, there wasn't a day that went by that her stepmother didn't scold her.

"**STUPID DORA!**" she'd shout...no matter what task was being done.

Dora and I were in her room at the nursing home. That frail 103-year-old woman was lying in her bed. Her skin was paper thin and her voice was quite feeble. It was obvious that the life energy running her body was slowly fading.

"**STUPID DORA! STUPID DORA!**" she repeated the monotonous statement.

All the while, I was trying to process the WHY behind that perpetual loop in her brain, that etched-out thought that dominated her mind—almost a century after the fact. It was amazing that after an entire lifetime of diverse events, the dominant thought she held on to was **STUPID DORA**.

I was fascinated by what I was listening to for the following reasons. Throughout my years of study on what makes successful, happy, people tick, I have repeatedly heard the following statements:

"Words are like arrows, once released we can't take them back."

"Put your mind in gear before you put your mouth in gear."

"You become what you think about most of the time. You are what your environment is."

"You'll become like the five closest people in your life."

I vividly remember my trip home, traveling south on the Henry Hudson Parkway, approaching the George Washington Bridge, deep in thought and recognizing how powerful our software program is.

As I conclude this story, I want you to reflect for a few minutes and ask yourself what **Stupid Dora** means to you. Where in your contemplations are you stuck? What's the one incessant "loop of thought" that dominates the precious minutes of your day? I often think of the total amount of time we consume on the repetitive thoughts that dominate ALL OF OUR LIVES. The way out of this prison is just to be aware of these contemplations and to know that we can choose new and empowering thoughts to take their place.

Do the work. Challenge yourself to identify the disempowering thoughts that rob you of precious minutes every day of your life. My wish is for all of us to learn from my Nanny that we CAN CHOOSE our thoughts and make awareness more important than the next desired article of clothing or some other purchase that will make life right for us.

THINK ABOUT THIS.

I want to thank my grandmother for all she taught me through her amazing lifetime. I've discovered that our pains are our lessons. We're infinitely connected, and my prayer is that this sharing supports others by the powerful message presented. This short story has the power to reach many people if shared with everyone. Be certain, if you plan on having children, never to demean them. **Words have the power to create wounds that never heal.**

As you go forward in your business and personal life, **STAY CONSCIOUS.** Do not default to "reflexive" answers. Slow your brain down to speak rationally.

Children form habits, and habits form their future. Be the model, not the critic. Remember, your children are born into this world with a "blank slate." That is, their minds are empty hard drives that receive data and store that data without judgment. Create a CONSCIOUS INTENTION to sow seeds of love, kindness, and empathy. Your offspring and the rest of the world will receive this blessing.

§

Chapter 8

Struggling to be OK

As I sit here this morning, reflecting over thirty-seven years of reading and writing, seminar giving, and talking about prosperity and success consciousness, I recognize how vulnerable I am to the never-ending quest of **feeling just good enough**.

Maybe the effort that I'm putting into learning and teaching this information has, at its root, my own feeling of inadequacy. After all, why would somebody want to spend countless hours a day, week after week, reading material that's fairly consistent from one text to the next? As I ponder this thought, I'm struck by how powerful our old program really is.

My analogy for recreating a new belief system is like trying to free yourself from the gravitational forces of this planet. NASA needs to spend billions of dollars in fuel to simply lift a rocket into space. The forces of gravity are so great that the actual rocket needs ninety percent kinetic energy to free itself from this force. So it is with our lives. We spend, or rather, expend, enormous amounts of energy trying to set ourselves free. Human beings do this by looking outside of themselves to make things right. We incessantly look to consume, to add to our menagerie of things and trinkets, and to make ourselves feel OK to our neighbors and friends.

From our earliest years, we've been subject to the software of consumption. If it's not newspaper and magazines, it's television shows that dramatize celebrities in a media centric society. The unfortunate circumstance is that the viewer only sees a snapshot view of the glorified idol, and rarely hears the whole story. Many critics blame the sign of the times as the causal factor. For instance, expressions like **the Mercedes '80s,** when the basic premise on t-shirts stated, **"He who dies with the most toys wins."** Yes, we could argue that it was just a sign of the times, yet how do we explain ancient Egypt, when the pharaohs were doing the same thing? They just took it one step further. Simply because the philosophy of *you can't take it with you* wasn't realized, they built pyramids, the older version of McMansions, where they stored all of their prized possessions, hoping to take it all with them in their next life.

So, welcome to the human dilemma. At least for now, humankind will continue with frustration, envy, jealousy, and a host of other negative qualities that prohibits them from enjoying life to its fullest. I think it would be fascinating to see a study of the amount of time we spend looking outside of us, feeling our level of inadequacy and comparing that to the amount of time we spend in pursuing a passion, a purpose, and simply **a life that matters**.

I love the expression that Gerry Spence uses in his book, *Seven Simple Steps to Personal Freedom*. He states: "Cages are cages, whether constructed of steel and concrete or from the fabric of the mind."

Pause for a moment and really contemplate what that last sentence means to you. Our cage is our limited ability to make sense and to give meaning to the events and circumstances of our lives. The only meaning anything has is the meaning you give to it.

§

"We were born with two fears—the fear of falling and the fear of loud noises. Every other fear you have was learned."

Chapter 9

Secret Conversations with Ourselves: The Haunting Space Between Your Ears

S top and consider for just one moment—wait, no—not one moment. This is deserving of more time. That's right, we spend an inordinate amount of time focused on everything outside the mind.

How much effort do you put into your hair, eyes, lips, body hair, clothing, accessories, car, or home?

Here's my point. If our thoughts generate our feelings, why do we spend so much time on our external being?

Answer: Because our concern for other's judgment of ourselves supersedes our own feeling of self.

The very essence of this book, as I contemplate this thought, is to help you move closer to joy, peace, and serenity.

The quantum world has shown us that there's a much bigger world of activity that goes on around us that's invisible.

Think about it. Cell phone signals, wi-fi, x-rays, satellite signals to all receivers, and last, but not least, your thoughts!

That's right, those invisible, non-tangible, non-audible stream of words, not heard by anyone but you.

Have you ever really stopped and evaluated these provocative concepts? What are those messages that only you contemplate and hear? Is it a repeated message that's on repeat mode?

Each of us recreates and reinvents secret images of how we wish we were. Many of these thoughts would create great embarrassment if others were to know them.

Our secret world, through our secret thoughts, is part of all of us—welcome again to being human.

For many of us, these thoughts consist of fantasies of how we can become rich and famous. Others fabricate meeting beautiful women or handsome men who seduce us. Others boil in a hate-filled world with bitterness and resentment over a life that just hasn't turned out the way we had hoped for.

More than anything, there doesn't seem to be any relief from this steady stream of negative thought that flows through our minds.

Or is there?

Self-introspection, the "examined life," or simply awareness are at least steps toward expressing more inward peace and harmony.

There's an expression: "We can't see ourselves as others see us. We're always looking outward and rarely inward."

So, what does all this mean to you?

First, I think that it's crucial for all of us to see our similarities. We suffer with the same illusions! We simply have the "volume" turned up on different areas of our life. Simply coming to the realization that it's not just you who experiences these thoughts, doubts, and negative vibrations should at least minimize your personal alienation.

Remember, we're all in this game together. When you learn to share your honest, heartfelt feelings with others, you demonstrate your authenticity. The more authentic you are as a person, the more welcomed and loved you are by almost everyone who knows you. You strengthen your own identity, not weaken it.

It reminds me of the distinction between our character and our personality. Think about this. Our personality is our "outside" portrayal. It's the button we push when we need to be "on." It's our make-believe traits that we must have "working" when we interact on a social or business communication. Our character is our "true nature," the part of our personality that's rooted in strong values and beliefs.

All too often, our personality can be manipulative or deceptive. We can choose to say things that "win over" somebody or make us liked in a given set of circumstances.

While we all have a character and a personality, it might be interesting to assess how congruent or incongruent these are in you. From an integrity point of view, the closer and more consistent the character and personality are, the greater will be trust and credibility felt by the other party.

In the words of William George Jordan, "Into the hands of every individual is given a marvelous power of good and evil. The silent unconscious, unseen influence of his life....

Is Your Lifestyle Killing You?

This is simply the constant radiation of what man really is, not what he pretends to be."

What is it that radiates from you? If you were to be so authentic right now, how would you show up each day at work and with your family and friends?

Remember, I need you to open your heart. Who is the authentic you?

Are you angry, bitter, and resentful, or grateful, supportive, nurturing, and loving?

While we all fluctuate with our emotions, which of the above stations are you most tuned into?

It's an important question, because regardless of what you mind says, it's your presence, your energy field that is felt by everyone around you. The old adage "words are cheap" rings so true. It's the **WHO YOU ARE**, not the **what you do and say** that reaches the hearts of your fellow human beings.

Wayne Dyer, the best-selling author and speaker, stated something very eloquent when he remarked, "We are born looking out when we should be looking within."

I remember being at a seminar when Harvey Cohen, Ph.D., remarked, "We have within us everything we need to know, whenever we need to know it."

Yet when most people are looking for answers, their desperation and lack of faith in themselves often drives them to look in the wrong places.

In concluding a chapter on "thought as things," I want you to carve out of your day 10–15 minutes as a sacred time to be with you. Within this daily ritual, it's imperative to acknowledge, either in the spoken word or in written form, all that you're grateful for. I want you to switch your favorite station on the radio from WIIFM (what's in it for me) to WIIFO (what's in it for others).

Victor Frankel, in his book, *Man's Search for Meaning*, marvelously demonstrated that man can be stripped of everything (clothes, dignity, and food), but regardless of the severity of dehumanization, nobody can control your thoughts. It was this strategy that helped him survive his horrific experience in the prison camps of Nazi Germany during WWII.

With this message, it's my hope and prayer that these few pages will make you think about the power you possess to retrain you mind and to apply the discipline of conscious thought. Live in this moment with intent to govern thoughts that empower yourself, give energy, life, and love to others. Like it or not, accept it or not, it's your choice. The gift is in you to own this.

§

"FACE YOUR FEAR! On the other side of FEAR lies your freedom."

Chapter 10

The Price
of Personal Vulnerability

M ost of us are protective of exposing our blemishes. No, not those blackheads and irritating red pimples that surface at the most inopportune times, but rather those deep-rooted imperfections about ourselves.

Does anyone really know that below the surface of this "designer man or woman" lies a failing relationship or a business that's hanging on for its life?

How often do we hear the expression, "That's only the tip of the iceberg?"

Let's talk Earth science for just one moment. An iceberg, like the one that devastated the Titanic, is a mass of frozen matter that exposes itself fractionally compared to its total size. In other words, 1/7th to 1/10th of its actual size lies above the water visible to the eye. The bulk of it lies hidden beneath the surface.

People, just like you and me, are icebergs of humanity. We will expose only a portion of the "who we are" for others to see. We often selectively reveal those parts of us that enhance our ego or demonstrate our "have" component—our acquisitions, accomplishments, or purchases. The vast percentage of our being lies deep below the surface, rarely to be seen by others.

My purpose of this chapter is to help you achieve more emotional freedom in order to say, "Will the real you please stand up?"

I want you to do so willingly, enthusiastically, and without hesitancy.

Now, I mean right now, do you have any idea of the weight you're carrying; the cost of psychic energy and its life depleting qualities?

Imagine yourself in a burlap bag, lying in a fetal position, and everywhere you went that day, you had to lift your satchel and throw it over your shoulder while sleeping or walking to your next meeting.

Metaphorically, this is what we do when we don't honor all "sides" of us. The expression, "no matter where you go, there you are" reminds us that we can't escape our own feelings of ourselves. Thus, when we lack authenticity, it's a burden that never goes away.

Think about the stories we've all heard over the years of people "coming out of the closet" to share their gay or lesbian realities and the talk of the incredible burden they've been carrying for years. This example is just one of many that so demonstrates how manifesting your authenticity creates emotional freedom and a sense of being whole.

> "To be yourself in a world that is constantly trying to make you something else is the greatest accomplishment."
> — *Ralph Waldo Emerson*

Interesting, isn't it, that we can sometimes spend a lifetime playing hide and seek? You thought you gave up that game when you graduated from fourth grade. Guess what? You didn't. You simply moved to the adult version.

Nobody wants to be rejected. That's one of the great fears involved with revealing ourselves to one another. We want respect, not rejection. Ironically, it has been my experience through my life that when you allow more visibility into your life by sharing real scenarios and honest feedback, rather than rejection, your rewards are deeper relationships and others opening their hearts to you.

The observation is that someone needs to be the initiator of vulnerability. Once the veil is opened, the other party wants to share more of their real feelings and experiences. Bottom line: it takes courage.

"What somebody else thinks of me is none of my business."

To understand the meaning of that statement is a wonderful start toward embracing your own authenticity. We can't control other people's opinions. Clarity of this brings you closer to living "your life." The more you live your own existence, the lighter the load will be. The problem for most of us is that we believe the person across the table is in a better place with their life than we are (financially, relationship-wise, etc.). We default, once again, to an illusion and an erroneous interpretation that often is incorrect and certainly disempowers us. Something to contemplate often is that regardless of what you share with others, you, and only you, know what's accurate, real, and above board. Therefore, who are we fooling, anyway?

"You may fool the whole world down the pathway of years and get pats on the back as you pass, but your final reward will be heartache and tears if you've cheated the man in the glass."

That's a powerful stanza to a very prophetic poem. It would be worth your while to sit down with a blank piece of paper and write down those things you often embellish, exaggerate, or just plain lie about!

§

"To be authentic is literally to be your own author...to discover your own natural energies and desires, and then to find your own way of acting on them."
— *Warren Bennis*

Chapter 11

Under the Influence of Money

A new paradigm is paramount for the next generation. I say this because as a health care practitioner, I've listened to hundreds of patients acknowledge how stress is "killing them." Although stress comes packaged in an infinite variety of ways, it's my contention that money is at the root of many stress factors.

Think about it. Most people are fixated on money. Once a student leaves high school or graduates from college, he or she is on the hunt for a paycheck. We all know how costly everything is, so getting by is our first challenge. Even if you happen to be one of the fortunate few who has excess dollars after expenses, you need to know what to do with this excess. TV and radio hammer our senses with messages like "ask Chuck." Yes, Charles Schwab is the man, yet if we read the

Motley Fool on the Web or listen to *Mad Money* on TV, we may hear a different lesson on financial fitness.

> "Do not value money for any more or less than its worth; it's a good servant but a bad master."
> — *Alexandre Dumas*

No matter where we are in life, there is that constant knot in the belly. How do I earn more? What do I do with what I earn? How do I hang onto it so it's there in the future? Finally, how do I share it with my loved ones when I die?

Shoot me! When do we have the time to live, to simply enjoy our simple pleasures like a walk in the woods, or a drive in the country?

I love the expression: **"When our outflow exceeds our income, then our upkeep becomes our downfall."**

Please read that again. Can you relate to those words? I surely can. When I think of my life during the '80s, I definitely resonate with that message!

Have you heard others (or yourself) say, "Where does it all go? No matter what I earn, no matter what my raises are, it gets all gobbled up."

I recommend you take a look at a wonderful book called *Your Money or Your Life*, by Joe Dominguez. It's a fabulous expose of how we trade off our life energy for money.

If your life is anything like mine, you'll agree that an enormous amount of time is consumed daily as we handle paperwork that directly or indirectly impact finances.

Ever involve yourself with a college loan? Is one of your favorite female friends Sallie Mae? Have you recently applied for a mortgage or any other financing?

Have you endeavored to help a loved one, grandparent, or parent to get into an assisted living facility or nursing home?

As a holistic health counselor, I know how important it is to work with the "whole person." Our emotions impact our physiology in a huge way. So it is with our finances. In most money management books and fiscal common sense literature, it is assumed that your financial life functions separately from the rest of your life. Once again, I want to wake you up from any potentially unconscious state you may be in and have you heed the following warning:

Your finances and the state of your financial condition are most often a mirror image of your life purpose and values.

"The great Western disease is 'I'll be happy when...when I get the money....when I get a BMW...when I get this job.'
Well, the reality is you never get to when. The only way to find happiness is to understand that happiness is not out there. It's in here. And happiness is not next week. It's now."
— *Marshall Goldsmith*

Take a good, hard, honest, and open look at your current state of affairs. If it's a "beautiful thing," I commend you. If it's causing you hives and reflux problems, I don't condemn you, but please let this be a wake up call to take action, and more importantly, to ask the question why?

Why is it so out of control?

What needs am I fulfilling by buying things I can't comfortably afford?

My intention behind this chapter is to help you get as honest as you can with yourself. The word success—how do you define it? Is your definition truly yours or are you simply using someone else's words?

Where has your own personal journey taken you? Most people I speak to and read about are in better shape financially than they've ever been in that they're earning more. However, the pressure of **maintaining this lifestyle** has been taking its toll on most of us.

Simply stated, over time our relationship with money—earning it, spending it investing it, owning it, protecting it, and worrying about it—has taken over the major part of our lives.

In our quest to create a good future for our kids, we work harder, become double income families, and thus relegate the rearing of our kids to daycare centers or nannies.

From my perspective, the material progress that was supposed to have freed us has left us more enslaved.

Since work occupies about 7/10th of our lives, a great question to ask yourself right now is, **"Am I making a living or am I making a dying?"**

Psychotherapist Douglas La Bier speaks about a "social disease" in his book *Modern Madness*. The steady stream of successful professionals who showed up in his office with exhausted bodies and empty souls alerted him to the mental and physical hazards of our regard for materialism. La Bier found that focusing on money, position, and success, at the expense of personal fulfillment and meaning, had led to sixty percent of his sample of several hundred to suffer from depression, anxiety, and often job-related disorders.

I could go on forever with quoted examples and personal life stories. For most people, clutter enters our lives through the "more is better" door. It comes from the modern disease of *materialism*. I define materialism as "looking for inner happiness or fulfillment in outer processions." It comes from the early programming that discomfort can be alleviated by something external—a baby bottle, a blanket, a bicycle, a BA, a BMW, or another kind of bottle.

I once read that there are two ways to be rich. One is to have more; the other is to want less. It isn't letting go of things that's important, but letting go of **attitudes toward things**.

What is fascinating about money isn't so much the entity itself, but our interpretation of it. For instance, there are millions of people who need not concern themselves with expenses like mortgages and bills. They have a great deal of extra money at their disposal, yet their consciousness is all about fear and loss. So they may have even more anxiety about money matters than someone or a family just getting by.

Are you getting my point? This subject is absolutely no different than any other "life area." Remember the statement that I used earlier in the book: It isn't the circumstances in our lives, it's our own interpretation that matters most."

"Man's many desires are like the small metal
coins he carries about in his pocket.
The more he has,
the more they weigh him down."
— *Satya Sai Baba*

Over and over again, it's my conviction that each of us
has to "go within" ourselves and revisit our interpretations
often. Without this step, we'll never get out of the "groove of
the vinyl record," so round and round we'll go.

Do you awaken with similar thoughts almost everyday?
Do you find yourself focused on similar, yet limited areas of
your life, such as a lack of money, lack of fulfillment, or lack
of appreciation?

Remember, little children rarely ever have this! The point
I'm making is that all of this is *learned*. We were programmed
to think this way, and therefore, we can reprogram the
program.

The intent of each chapter is to raise your awareness.
When you spend uninterrupted time asking and answering
these questions, you'll be moving away from your head and
toward your heart. Take the few minutes to ponder these
points. Conscious thought will energize and take you out
of the stupor that most of us live in. The pressure cooker
of hunting for the next morsel of consumption, hoping that
the next acquisition will make it better, is exhausting and

unfulfilling. This is a disease that becomes an emotional malignancy, as we get caught up in "society's game."

Consciousness and awareness are the most profound antidotes to the festering germs that come at us from every direction. Open up any magazine or newspaper. What is the dominant filler of these pages? Advertisements. They're all hawking for your dollar. In order to look better, to feel better, or to keep up with others, buy me, buy me, buy me!

Fast forward. It's been twenty years since you entered the job market. You have a home with everything in it. Your garage, your basement, and your attic are all filled with remnants and artifacts of things that promised you happiness, fulfillment, and a sense of *I'm OK because I own it*. Stuff! What do most people say upon looking at all of this?

Well, I've heard, "Get rid of it! Clutter—everywhere I look I have stuff I never use, will never use, and I just want to get rid of it!"

Wait a minute! This was the stuff you absolutely needed! What's even more frustrating, some of the things we're talking about are still being paid off.

What does all of this mean? Money is a very powerful, unexplored thread in our lives and work. It's critical for all of us to take inventory of the interpretations and symbolic meanings we've given to money. Remember, like every other belief system we carry in us, impressions about money began at a very early age.

Please take the next few pages to write your own story about your personal relationship with money. Ultimately, what I've learned is to accept what is, as is.

Let life be. If you can learn to make money ordinary and not give it imagined power, your life can become more peaceful and serene—something we all want, something we can't put a price tag on.

May this chapter help you move from a state of relentless pursuit to living a life filled with love, appreciation, and meaning. Remember, the only meaning anything has is the meaning YOU give it.

§

"Happiness cannot be traveled to, owned, earned, worn, or consumed. Happiness is the spiritual exercise of living every minute with love, grace, and gratitude."
— *Dennis Waitley*

Chapter 12

Life's Mulligan

If you've never played golf, you may have no idea what a Mulligan is. Let me help and give you a definition. When a friendly game of golf is played among friends, each golfer is given a second chance to hit their first shot off the tee. Understand that hitting a golf ball straight is as difficult as living a "fulfilled life."

Most of us have fantasized about having a chance to do life over again. Thus the expression "if I only knew then what I know now." Have you ever heard that one? Have you ever spoken that one?

Well, this fantasy is really not that far-fetched. Although we can't hit the "rewind" button on our lives, we can hit the "pause" button.

I want to take you to an imaginary place for just a moment. It's called the **GAP**. You visit it hundreds of times a day, and rarely recognize it. It's a powerful place that resides between a stimulus and a response. It's where we contemplate what just happened, the stimulus, and the action we then took, the response. It's in this moment that our nervous system communicates with our head (logic), heart (values), and reflexes (innate response), and collectively decides how to respond. Sometimes it's a millisecond, other times it can be minutes, hours, or even a lifetime of contemplation.

Please spend a few minutes with me. How many of your responses to your children, co-workers, or spouses are thought through? How many are simply reflexive answers? This might be a wonderful time to consider the GAP and see how a bit more empathy and understanding may serve these relationships. It's worth taking another inventory. Put the book down and consider how many responses you use in the course of a day are mimicked words you heard growing up. Do these serve the relationships? Do they honor the other person in front of you? The GAP is hugely important and I hope you revisit this concept often. It could alter the quality of your life in proportions unimaginable.

The Mulligan I'm metaphorically speaking about is the life you can begin to live, starting this very moment. It's simply a choice; a decision not to make tomorrow a carbon copy of today.

Here's what I'm suggesting:

Ask yourself: What were the five most powerful concepts you derived or extracted from this book?

Write them down.

Secondly, get a pen and paper, and get to work to ensure that you "lift that needle out of the vinyl groove." Let's face it, you and I have read many a book prior to this one, and we were inspired or moved by some concepts or ideas.

The questions to raise are: Were the changes you made permanent? Did you make any changes?

To know and not to "do" is really not to know at all.
To assist you in this most important assignment to create another chance (Mulligan) to live a more inspired, enriched, and appreciated life, I'd like to share my *ah-ha's!* and reflect on conscious changes I put into place that altered my own life considerably.

As I look into the rearview mirror of my life, I now recognize that I often lived out the desires of other people in my life more than my own.

I got caught up in a lifestyle of my neighborhood, which was at times beyond my own personal comfort level, yet in an effort to prove my self-worth and net worth, I leveraged more than what I should have and spent countless hours, days, and years frustrated with the choices. It's interesting that the frustration level was much greater and long lasting than whatever gratification that came from any of my acquisitions.

Each of us is given an opportunity to experience the "second shot."

I'll be bold enough to say that we're given this opportunity at every given second that we're alive. That's right—it takes only one second for our nervous system to recognize that something isn't right. It's a bigger acknowledgement to DO SOMETHING!

Our willingness to risk change and confront our old ways is where boldness and genius begin.

Life doesn't end after completing this book. You may choose to reread the book in its entirety, or you might go to a specific chapter. Whatever road you take once you finish this text, I want to send you off with a prayer:

May you awaken the little voice inside of you that recognizes your incredible unique gift. Remind yourself to give yourself a hug and a pat on the back—you deserve that.

You aren't in this world to live up to anyone else's expectations, but to **live out all that you are**.

You were placed on this planet to serve others, not to adorn yourself. Your value is expressed when you support and nurture others. Your life will be fuller with joy and fulfillment when you let go of **me** and think of **we**.

Finally, like a tree or anything in nature, you'll grow as big as your genetic potential will allow you to. Discard the limiting beliefs that others place on you. Society is a disease. Grow quiet each and every day and listen to the gentle whispers of your heart. Trust in the messages that come from this source. Question everything that comes from everywhere else.

Does all this sound like too much work?

Remember, you're in the groove of a vinyl record, and the only person who can lift the needle is you.

Listen, to the sound of music you're playing right now...

That's your song—your life. If you love the lyrics, the background, and the instruments, just let it keep on playing.

If you think you can sweeten the words, enhance the harmony, and deliver a better message, then go for it. There's no higher calling and nothing more satisfying than living **your life**.

I believe in you and I know you can.

"Play it again." You have a second chance. It all begins right now!

The Man in the Glass

When you get what you want in your
struggle for self
And the world makes you king for a day,
Just go to the mirror and look at yourself
And see what the man has to say.
For it isn't your father or mother or wife
Whose judgment upon you must pass
The fellow whose verdict counts most
in your life
Is the one staring back from the glass.
Some people may think you
a straight-shootin' chum,
And call you a wonderful guy,
But the man in the glass says
you're only a bum,
If you can't look him straight in the eye.
He's the fellow to please,
never mind all the rest
For he's with you clear up to the end
And you've passed your most dangerous
difficult test
If the man in the glass is your friend.
You may fool the whole world
down the pathway of years
And get pats on the back as you pass,
But your final reward will be
heartache and tears
If you've cheated the man in the glass.
—*Author Unknown*

About Dr. Chuck Berg

A successful chiropractor for 37 years, a student and teacher of integrative nutrition and now a speaker, author and executive lifestyle coach, Chuck Berg has brought his message of wellness and balance to clients as diverse as BMW North America, UBS Financial Services the International Council for Women in Real Estate and listeners of his "Reclaiming Your Health" radio show. Chuck offers a rich understanding of the value of a life transformed from the inside out—one where equal attention is paid to the physical, the relational, the spiritual and the mindful. As a professional life skill coach, Chuck's message to busy professionals is clear: your work performance will be in exact proportion to your energy, vitality and emotional and physical health.

Chuck, in his 37-year practice, observed that even highly successful people were living life completely out of balance and weren't in a position to enjoy what they were creating. This recurring pattern led him to create this book which recognizes the high stress levels of the work force and allows them to honestly evaluate their life. Combining the knowledge of exercise physiology, nutrition and personal development skills, Chuck demonstrates how succeeding on an emotional and physical level is equally if not more important than economic gain alone.

"I love being a coach and an agent of change," adds Chuck. "Whether I am speaking to a large audience of employees at a Fortune 500 corporation, or one patient in my office, I challenge each person to examine their belief systems and values. I like to give people the opportunity to question habits and create a new strategy that comes from their own personal aspirations and new empowering choices.

Made in the USA
Middletown, DE
22 December 2015